SAM ILLINGWORTH
KIRSTEN JACK

POETRY AND PEDAGOGY IN HIGHER EDUCATION

A Creative Approach to Teaching, Learning, and Research

First published in Great Britain in 2024 by

Policy Press, an imprint of
Bristol University Press
University of Bristol
1–9 Old Park Hill
Bristol
BS2 8BB
UK
t: +44 (0)117 374 6645
e: bup-info@bristol.ac.uk

Details of international sales and distribution partners are available at
policy.bristoluniversitypress.co.uk

British Library Cataloguing in Publication Data
A catalogue record for this book is available from the British Library

ISBN 978-1-4473-7229-5 hardcover
ISBN 978-1-4473-7231-8 ePub
ISBN 978-1-4473-7230-1 ePdf

Cover design: Bristol University Press
Front cover image: Unsplash/Clark Young

Contents

List of tables

Glossary

Authentic assessment: Forms of assessment that require students to apply knowledge and skills to practical contexts, problems, and performances, evaluating higher-order skills beyond just recall of facts. Poetry assignments can serve as authentic assessments.

Blackout poetry: A poetic technique where an existing text is transformed into a poem by selectively redacting words.

Epistemology: The philosophy of knowledge, dealing with how we know things and what we can regard as knowledge. A constructivist epistemology, which emphasises that understanding is subjective and constructed from lived experiences rather than externally acquired, aligns well with the use of poetry in research.

Experiential learning: The process of learning through direct experience and reflecting on that experience. Poetry can be used to enhance reflection and meaning making from experiences.

Formative assessment: Assessment activities that provide ongoing feedback to students during the learning process to guide improvement. Useful scaffolding strategies like peer reviews of poem drafts act as formative assessment.

Found poetry: A poetic form created by selecting compelling words and phrases from existing texts and rearranging them into a poem. Can be used as an innovative literature review format.

Interpersonal intelligence: The ability to understand other people, relate to them and interact effectively. Poetry can help to build this empathy and communication skill.

Intrapersonal intelligence: The ability to understand yourself, your emotions, strengths, weaknesses, motivations, and desires. Poetry aids development of this self-knowledge.

Ontology: The study of the nature of reality and existence. A relativist ontology which posits multiple subjective realities aligns with poetic perspectives.

Pedagogy: The method and practice of teaching, incorporating theories of education, psychology, sociology, and ethics.

Poetic autoethnography: Blends poetry writing and personal narrative as a means of researcher reflexivity, using autobiographical poems to provide insights into the researcher's experiences.

Poetic inquiry: A qualitative research method using poetry writing and analysis throughout the research process, from data collection to presentation of findings.

Poetic transcription: A research method that transforms qualitative data sources like interview transcripts into poetic form to highlight key emotions, ideas, and experiences.

Problem-based learning: A student-centred pedagogy where students learn through collaboratively solving open-ended problems.

Reflection: The process of critically thinking about experiences, actions, and beliefs to gain self-knowledge and make improvements. Poetry nurtures insightful reflection.

Reflexivity: The process of critically examining and reflecting on one's own biases, perspectives, and assumptions and how these affect research or practice. Poetic methods like autoethnography can enable educator reflexivity.

Rubric: A scoring guide detailing expectations for a task or assessment through a set of criteria and gradations of quality.

Scaffolding: Instructional supports provided to students to facilitate learning and success with new material or challenging tasks. Useful in introducing poetry to build confidence.

Summative assessment: Evaluation of learning and achievement at the conclusion of an instructional period, such as through final exams or papers. Poetry can also be used for summative assessment.

UDL (Universal Design for Learning): A framework promoting inclusive and accessible education through multiple means of representation, engagement, and expression.

Validity: In research, whether a method accurately measures what it aims to measure. Poetry research can demonstrate validity through documentation, auditing, and contextualisation.

Acknowledgements

Our journey in writing this book has been underpinned by the unwavering support and encouragement of our families, whose patience and understanding have been our constant companions. To them, we extend our deepest gratitude for being the bedrock upon which this work stands.

We also extend our heartfelt appreciation to our colleagues and students in the world of higher education. The rich tapestry of knowledge and experiences you have shared with us over the years has not only enriched our perspectives but has been instrumental in shaping the contents of this book.

Our sincere thanks are extended to Bristol University Press for bringing this book to life, with a special mention to Paul Stevens and Isobel Green. Your insightful guidance and unwavering support throughout this process have been invaluable.

The constructive critiques of our anonymous reviewers have been a compass in refining and perfecting this work. Their keen insights and thoughtful feedback have greatly contributed to the depth and quality of this book.

Finally, we would like to express our gratitude to Leslie Almberg, Patricia Hemminger, Doryn Herbst, Anna Joyce, Jairo Rincon, Magaret Sivapragasam, and Niina Turtola. Your generous review and insightful suggestions on our earlier drafts have been invaluable in shaping the final manuscript.

ONE

Poetry in the higher education landscape

Chapter highlights

- Introduction to the transformative potential of poetry in higher education.
- The benefits of integrating poetry across disciplines.
- Strategies to overcome challenges and resistance in incorporating poetry.
- Case studies demonstrating the effective use of poetry in various subjects.
- Discussion on the future of poetry in higher education.

Introduction

In the bustling halls of academia, the trinity of speed, performativity, and standardisation has emerged as the driving force, a beacon guiding the trajectory of modern higher education (Ramsden, 2003). Yet, like a chorus echoing in the amphitheatres of ancient Greece, a burgeoning sense of creativity, individuality, and diversity continues to permeate these, at times, lofty and exclusionary edifices of learning.

Speed is seen by many as pivotal in the current academic landscape. It mirrors our rapidly changing society, our swift intellectual evolution, and the expeditious transmission of knowledge that technology has brought forth (Sarauw and Madsen, 2020). Institutions are being pushed to adopt this pace, to synchronise with the rhythm of progress. Yet, in this march towards haste, we risk leaving behind the deep-rooted scholarly traditions of reflection, contemplation, and rigorous discourse, components that make up the very DNA of academia (Berg and Seeber, 2016).

Performativity, too, looms large in our educational ethos, encapsulating the drive towards efficiency, demonstrable productivity, and tangible outcomes (Macfarlane, 2015). Both educators and learners find themselves gauged by a relentless tide of metrics: grades, publications, employment statistics, and so forth. However, let us not forget that the essence of learning often thrives in that which is unseen and immeasurable, in the crucible of critical thought, resilience, and empathy (English, 2016).

Similarly, standardisation, while ensuring a level of uniformity and equity, might inadvertently stifle the spirit of creativity and individualism (De Vita and Case, 2003). Higher education, ideally, is a vibrant mosaic of diverse experiences, ideas, and approaches. The beauty lies not in their uniformity but in their difference, the unique fragments that coalesce to form a holistic, enriching experience for all.

It is within this stifling trinity that poetry emerges as an unlikely liberator. Surprising in its manifestation, yet potent in its impact, poetry offers a pathway towards individuality and diversity within the structured frameworks of higher education. It becomes a conduit for personal expression, a space where learners and educators alike can explore nuanced perspectives, challenge preconceptions, and revel in the richness of human experience.

That is the purpose of this book: to illuminate the transformative potential of poetry within higher education.

By transcending the traditional parameters of speed, performativity, and standardisation, we enter the poetic realm, to foster (and celebrate) creativity, individuality, and diversity. Geared towards those engaged with or situated in higher education, this book offers an invitation to discover the unique blend of structured learning and artistic expression that poetry provides. Through practical strategies and vivid examples, we will explore the many ways poetry can enrich teaching and learning experiences, stimulating reflection, empathy, and personal growth.

Each chapter unfolds to reveal a different aspect of this environment, brought to life through case studies exemplifying challenges, effective practices, and transformative approaches. Similarly, exercises invite you to explore and apply the concepts discussed, while suggestions for further study open doors to expanding your knowledge and understanding of the nexus of poetry and education. In all these exercises, we aim to share some guidance, although you will know best how to introduce poetry into your specific practice, based on issues such as the makeup of your learners, how well you know them, and what you want to achieve. In other words, feel free to use the steps that we present as a flexible guide, rather than an instruction manual.

But who are we? And why should you entrust us to be your guides on this journey?

We are Sam Illingworth and Kirsten Jack, academics and individuals profoundly impacted by the transformative power of poetry in both our professional and personal lives.

Sam comes from a scientific background where accuracy and precision are paramount. However, he has found that poetry, with its ability to touch hearts and open minds, is an invaluable tool for communicating complex scientific concepts. Over the years, he has explored this unlikely intersection of science and poetry, leading to significant revelations about the power of poetry to engage, inspire, and enlighten (Illingworth, 2021, 2022, 2023a).

Kirsten's professional path is rooted in nursing education, a field which often grapples with emotional resilience and reflection. Her experience has shown how the emotional resonance of poetry can encourage these essential qualities in health and social care professionals. The symbiotic relationship between nursing and poetry, with its capacity to express profound emotional truths, has been an enduring part of her teaching methodology and research (Jack, 2015, 2017, 2022).

Poetry, in our personal lives, has been a source of solace, a challenge, and an avenue for authentic self-expression. It has facilitated our understanding of and connection with the world in a genuinely profound manner. Thus, with our shared passion and unique intersections with poetry, we are well-positioned to guide you through this exploration of incorporating poetry into higher education. We are committed to highlighting how poetry, often overlooked in educational settings, can invigorate learning, stimulate creativity, and foster a more engaging, inclusive environment.

How to use this book

This book is designed as a resource for educators, practitioners, and learners who are keen on weaving poetry into the tapestry of higher education. It serves as a bridge between the structured rigour of academia and the liberating essence of poetic expression. Here is a guide on how to navigate this book to make the most of its content with regards to your own learning and teaching journey:

1. **Exploration.** Begin by immersing yourself in the first two chapters, which lay down the premise of integrating poetry into higher education. These sections will provide you with the theoretical grounding and the rationale behind this interdisciplinary approach.
2. **Engagement.** Each chapter unfolds a different facet of how poetry intersects with higher education, illustrated

through examples and exercises. Engage with these exercises, either individually or in a collaborative setting, to explore the concepts discussed. They are crafted to stimulate reflection, creativity, and a deeper understanding of the subject matter.

3. **Customisation.** The exercises and strategies presented are flexible. Adapt them to suit the unique needs and dynamics of your educational setting. Whether you are an educator aiming to invigorate your teaching methods, a practitioner seeking to enrich your practice, or a learner aspiring to deepen your understanding, tailor the exercises to meet your objectives.
4. **Discussion and reflection.** At the end of each chapter, take time to reflect on what you have learned, and if possible, engage in discussions with peers. Sharing insights and experiences can further enhance your understanding and application of the concepts explored.
5. **Exploring further.** At the end of each chapter, suggestions for further study are provided to fuel your continued exploration of the topics discussed. These resources are stepping stones to a broader understanding and deeper engagement with the synergies between poetry and higher education.

This book is designed to be a dynamic resource for educators and learners alike, offering insights into the integration of poetry in higher education. To enhance this process, each chapter begins with a set of bullet points summarising key content and themes. These bullets serve as quick references, enabling you to easily navigate through the book, identify relevant sections, and revisit specific topics as needed. They provide an accessible overview, making it simpler to assimilate the material and apply the ideas in various educational settings. Whether you are dipping in for specific guidance or exploring the book more thoroughly, these summaries aim to orient and enrich your reading experience.

Accessible and inclusive poetry

Poetry in higher education can be a powerful conduit for inclusivity, provided it is framed and delivered in a manner that resonates with all learners. It offers a unique platform for voices that might otherwise go unheard and experiences that are often left unacknowledged. This book, with its diverse range of exercises, aims to democratise the teaching and writing of poetry, ensuring it is a tool for all, not just a few. Through these exercises, we aspire to contribute to an inclusive academic dialogue where poetry enhances learning, mindful of the diversity in our classrooms. For each exercise, consider different learners and environments, to make poetry an accessible part of higher education for a broad audience.

For example, well-chosen poetry written by poets from varied backgrounds and cultures can enable consideration of implicit biases and support the broadening of perspectives. Poetry can enable us to consider how our own experiences and voices differ from those we read. We can choose poetry which helps us to identify challenges within our disciplines, which affect diverse groups and can subsequently inform our reflections and broaden the scope of our analysis. Poetry in all its forms and themes will resonate with the different people in your groups(s) and ensure the content is relevant and engaging for all. Selecting a diverse range of materials that encompass different perspectives, especially from underrepresented voices in the field, can foster a more comprehensive and inclusive understanding of the chosen topic.

When planning to use poetry in your teaching, consider the unique dynamics of your classroom environment, for example, the size of your class, whether your teaching is conducted remotely or face-to-face, and the diverse learning needs of your students. These factors play a crucial role in how accessible poetic materials and activities will be. For larger classes, digital platforms may be necessary for sharing poems and collecting reflections, while smaller groups might benefit from more interactive discussions or practical activities. In remote learning scenarios, ensure that technology is used effectively to engage all students with the poetry. Think about how you will adapt your teaching methods to suit the specific needs of your learners, so that poetry enhances the learning experience rather than presenting obstacles.

For larger classes, consider breaking students into smaller groups for discussion, and offer alternative ways for students to share their insights, such as written responses or digital forums, to accommodate those who may be less comfortable with verbal discussion. Ensure the materials are accessible in various formats, considering the diverse needs of students, such as providing digital versions of poems for screen readers or audio recordings for those with visual impairments.

As you embark on the exercises within these pages, please regard the suggested timings as a flexible framework, meant to guide rather than dictate the pace of learning. They are adjustable to suit the rhythm of each reader and the unique tempo of their different learning environments. Whether your setting is a traditional classroom, a virtual space, or a hybrid model, feel free to adapt these exercises to the resources at your disposal and the specific needs of your students.

The case for poetry in higher education

Poetry has long graced the classrooms of primary and secondary education, playing a significant role in language acquisition, creativity stimulation, and the development of emotional intelligence (Carter, 2013; Parker et al, 2009; Fiore, 2015). Yet, when we advance into higher education, the presence of poetry starts to wane, with its essence often concealed within the cloisters of literature studies and creative writing courses. But what if we allowed the rhythm of poetry to echo freely across the diverse fields of all subjects that are taught in higher education?

Let us traverse history a moment. The earliest universities were fundamentally different entities from today's institutions, with most of them born out of the monastic tradition of combining spiritual reflection with intellectual exploration (Haskins, 2002). Here, creativity was considered not just as an extracurricular flourish but as an inherent component of deep thinking and learning. Poetry, with its propensity to condense grand ideas into compact, digestible morsels, served as a potent vehicle for scholarly discourse (Marrou, 1982).

Fast forward to our modern academies. In the sprint towards employability, standardisation, and quantitative benchmarks, the 'slow' practice of poetry could be seen as a luxury or, worse still, an inefficiency. This is a deeply unfortunate misconception, as poetry can offer a plethora of benefits that can enhance traditional pedagogical approaches. From fostering critical thinking and emotional exploration to cultivating empathy and social justice awareness, the integration of poetry into higher education has shown promise across a multitude of disciplines (Camangian, 2008; Roberts, 2010; Illingworth, 2023b).

Moreover, poetry offers a salve for the modern malaise of 'information overload'. The abstraction of poetry encourages learners to engage with material in a personal, introspective way, fostering deeper understanding (Creely, 2018). By de-emphasising rote learning and prioritising experiential understanding, we can make strides towards a more comprehensive approach to education that balances knowledge acquisition with emotional intelligence and creative capacity.

EXERCISE 1.1: EXPLORING YOUR RELATIONSHIP WITH POETRY

Estimated engagement time: 60–90 minutes.

Aim: To foster a deeper understanding and appreciation of personal experiences with poetry.

Objectives:

- Identify past encounters with poetry outside the classroom setting.
- Analyse the impact of these encounters on personal perceptions of poetry.
- Discover personal preferences in poetry regarding styles, themes, and poets.

Output: A reflective narrative or journal entry detailing personal encounters and preferences in poetry.

Type of exercise: Individual.

Materials needed:

- Writing materials (pen and paper or digital device).
- Access to a variety of poems (optional for Step 4).

Activity:

Step 1: Remember early poetry encounters

Think back to your first significant encounters with poetry. Think beyond the classroom context and consider any memorable experiences you have had with poetry, whether it be through family, friends, or personal exploration. Was this poetry encountered in books, performances, or even overheard in conversation?

Step 2: Recall impactful experiences

Reflect on any especially meaningful experiences you have had with poetry so far. What made them stand out to you?

Step 3: Analyse favourite poems

If you have a favourite poem, examine what specific elements draw you to it. Is it the language, themes, imagery? How does it connect to you?

Step 4: Find a new favourite

If you do not have a favourite poem yet, explore some different styles and poets until you find one that connects with you personally. You may need to try a variety of styles, themes, or poets to find what resonates with you (see the section 'The future of poetry in higher education' for an idea of where to start). Remember, it is okay if not every poem speaks to you; that's part of the journey!

In the current higher education landscape, poetry is perceived by many as a fringe entity. Its widespread presence and impact on a broader scale are underappreciated, with a handful of exceptions in more exploratory disciplines or innovative teaching practices. A closer look at the literature reveals that the integration of poetry in pedagogy, albeit under-used, provides a substantial range of benefits across a wide range of academic disciplines.

Within humanities courses, particularly English literature and linguistics, the place of poetry is undisputed. Students are encouraged to read, analyse, and interpret poetic texts as part of their curriculum. These activities help them improve their language proficiency, understanding of literary devices, and ability to think critically. In this context, poetry is appreciated for its aesthetic, linguistic, and cultural value, cultivating students' skills in literary criticism and analysis (Simecek and Rumbold, 2016).

However, moving beyond the humanities, the application of poetry becomes sparse. Traditionally 'hard' disciplines such as science, technology, engineering, and mathematics (STEM) tend to view poetry as extraneous to their learning needs. Yet, several innovative educators and practitioners have challenged this view by effectively using poetry to elucidate complex scientific concepts, foster critical thinking, and facilitate deeper engagement with course materials (Brown, 2015; Ostrom et al, 2020).

For example, Rule et al (2004) describe an innovative teaching approach where a high school Earth science teacher and a university education professor collaboratively delivered a lesson to high school students, blending poetry with science to explore minerals. Through this method, not only does the curriculum extend beyond traditional content knowledge or process skills, but it also cultivates creativity and affective skills among the students. About half of the students also changed their perceptions of Earth science because of this poetic exploration.

Similarly, a study by Pollack and Korol (2013) illustrates how poetry can be used to convey complex concepts in neuroscience. Undergraduate students were tasked with composing a haiku that encapsulated the core traits of the neurological ailments examined in the course. Upon reflecting on this task, they noted that the constraints of constructing a haiku significantly honed their consideration of word selection and conceptualisation, more so than any other writing assignment in the class. Using such a creative approach to disseminate complex scientific concepts allows students to engage with, reflect on, and better understand the critical challenges facing our world.

A burgeoning body of research in medical humanities further emphasises the role of poetry in fostering empathy, reflection, and emotional resilience among medical students and professionals (Shapiro et al, 2006a; Maretic and Abbey, 2021). In this context, poetry provides a conduit for introspection and empathy, nurturing the emotional intelligence required when caring for others.

There is also emerging recognition of the benefits of including poetry within the curricula of business and economics education. Poetic devices like metaphor, imagery, and rhythm can help students grasp abstract concepts, inspire creativity, and stimulate robust discussion about contemporary business issues (Morris et al, 2005; Celly, 2009). Similarly, the poems of Charles Reznikoff (a 20th-century American lawyer) have been used to help teach law students how to paraphrase effectively (Nilon, 2020), with poetry also used in financial and managerial accounting courses as a unique tool to both enrich and evaluate student learning (Krom and Williams, 2011).

Despite these promising applications, a systemic change integrating poetry across the higher education spectrum remains slow. This hesitancy may in part stem from entrenched notions about the utilitarian value of education, prioritising practical, employable skills over creative, reflective ones (Giroux, 2020). However, the long-term push for greater creativity, emotional intelligence, and critical thinking in graduate attributes (Barnett, 2000) suggests the need for a broader, more inclusive educational approach where poetry has a vital role to play.

EXERCISE 1.2: CHALLENGES IN YOUR FIELD

Estimated engagement time: 90–120 minutes.

Aim: To raise awareness of significant challenges within your academic discipline, and to envision innovative approaches towards approaching these challenges.

Objectives:

- Articulate core challenges within your academic discipline.
- Analyse alternative perspectives or methods that might address these challenges.
- Document reflections for future reference and reassessment.

Output: A document detailing identified challenges within your field and potential innovative approaches towards them.

Type of exercise: Individual.

Materials needed:

- Writing materials (pen and paper or digital device).
- Any relevant academic literature or resources that may aid in reflection.

Activity:

Step 1: Reflect on your discipline

Set aside dedicated time to carefully reflect on your specific field. Make a list of the core concepts, abstract ideas, technical elements, or terminology that you find most difficult to fully comprehend or explain clearly to others. Try to dig beneath the surface to identify the root of these challenges.

Step 2: List the challenges

Review your reflections and choose two or three of the most significant challenges or obstacles. Write these down, articulating precisely why each one is so problematic or confusing for you. Be as specific as possible in defining the issue.

Step 3: Imagine new approaches

For each defined challenge, brainstorm at least one of two new perspectives, insights, metaphors, or tactics that could help reframe or tackle it in an innovative way. Let your mind wander freely, writing down any idea without judgement on its viability.

Step 4: Record your thoughts

Collect your notes into a document, carefully detailing each specific challenge and your ideas for reconsidering it. Make sure to save this in a secure place you can return to later.

Step 5: Return and reassess

Make a note of these challenges and return to them as you progress through the book, reflecting on how poetry might offer some potential solutions or at least alternative ways of viewing.

Addressing the challenges

Incorporating poetry into higher education can seem a daunting task. Several challenges can surface, from deeply rooted scepticism within the community to a scarcity of resources, or even the perceived incompatibility of poetry with certain disciplines. Despite these obstacles, we believe that the benefits of integrating poetry into the curriculum far outweigh these initial hurdles. To demonstrate this, let us explore these challenges in more detail.

Firstly, resistance from the educational community can be substantial. This is often grounded in the well-trod dichotomy between the sciences and the arts, a divide that dates at least to C.P. Snow's 'Two Cultures' debate (Snow, 2012) from the 1950s. Higher education institutions have been slow to bridge this gap, and some academics view any attempt to integrate arts-based practices such as poetry into 'serious' academic teaching as trivialising, or as a deviation from rigorous scientific or scholarly methods. But such resistance may also stem from the lack of exposure to the potential benefits poetry can offer in an educational setting. As practitioners and educators in higher education, we can play a crucial role in challenging this perspective. As discussed previously, an increasing body of literature supports the use of poetry as an educational tool across disciplines, from the humanities to the sciences. Poetry has been shown to stimulate creative thinking, enhance reflective practice, foster empathy, and promote a deeper understanding of complex topics (Webster, 2010; Chan, 2013; Wardle and Illingworth, 2022).

Secondly, a lack of resources can pose another significant barrier. Many educators may wish to incorporate poetry into their teaching but feel hindered by limited resources or a lack of personal competence in this area. However, this challenge can be mitigated through collaboration and the sharing of expertise. For instance, institutions can encourage partnerships between departments, such as humanities and sciences, to co-create interdisciplinary modules that integrate poetry (Ostrom et al, 2020). Workshops and seminars led by experienced practitioners can likewise empower educators to use poetry effectively, building on existing effective practices (Furman, 2014).

Finally, the perceived incompatibility of poetry with certain disciplines needs to be considered. Disciplines traditionally viewed as being more analytical or data-driven, such as mathematics or computer science, may see little relevance in integrating poetry. However, the power of poetry lies in its ability to evoke emotional responses and stimulate lateral thinking, both of which can enhance the understanding and appreciation of any subject (Osowiecka and Kolańczyk, 2018). For example, computer code can be seen as a form of poetry, with its own rhythm and structure (Marino, 2020). Teaching computer science students to view code from this perspective can potentially stimulate creativity, enhance critical thinking skills, and deepen their appreciation of the discipline.

Change can be daunting but is often the catalyst for innovation. By empathising with our colleagues' concerns and demonstrating the potential benefits, we can play a key role in promoting a more creative, inclusive, and empathetic approach to using poetry in higher education.

In considering the scepticism within the educational community, we need to understand but also empathise with these concerns. Academics are often expected to uphold standards of rigour, criticality, and traditional pedagogical principles, making it difficult to stray from established methods. Yet the landscape of higher education is continually evolving. Akin to other sectors, higher education must be able to adapt and innovate, responding to societal changes and students' diverse needs. Poetry offers a valuable tool in this regard (Simecek and Rumbold, 2016) however, we must make clear to colleagues exactly what the benefits of poetry are and how they can be realised and measured.

Regarding the lack of resources, we must strive to foster a culture of collaborative resource creation and sharing. As educators, we have an excellent opportunity to contribute to the wider academic community by creating and disseminating teaching materials that integrate poetry. Such efforts would not only benefit individual educators but could also lead to the establishment of collaborative networks spanning different disciplines and institutions. This idea aligns with the increasingly prevalent notion of Open Educational Resources (OERs), in which educators create and share teaching and learning materials openly, allowing others to use, adapt, and build upon their work (Wiley et al, 2014). With the growing importance of interdisciplinary studies and the global shift towards open education, such networks could play a crucial role in supporting educators wishing to incorporate poetry into their practice.

To address the perception of poetry being irrelevant in certain fields, we must extend our understanding of what poetry is and what it can do. Poetry is not confined to the traditional formats we often associate it with; it is a form of communication that allows for the expression of complex ideas and emotions in a condensed and evocative form. By promoting this broader understanding of poetry, we can challenge the perceived dichotomy between poetry and other disciplines, enhancing students' learning experiences. Doing so has the additional benefit of helping to diversify poetry and to move away from exclusive and exclusionary definitions of what is and is not a poem. In adopting this inclusive approach, we base our definition of poetry on that of Illingworth (2022):

> A poem does not have to rhyme, but all poems have rhythm.

We acknowledge that incorporating poetry into higher education can be challenging. However, by understanding these challenges, empathising with those who resist, and leveraging available resources, we can navigate these obstacles and reap the benefits that poetry offers. As we progress through this book, we will continue to explore ways of integrating poetry into higher education settings, demonstrating through case studies and practical exercises how poetry can support learners and educators alike in fostering creativity, empathy, and a deeper understanding of their subject matter.

Potential strategies and case studies

As we move deeper into the conversation about the potential of poetry within higher education, the next logical step is to discuss strategies for its integration and to consider case studies that illustrate its successful implementation. The worth of any theoretical proposition is found in its practical applicability. In doing so we want to ensure that this book is not merely a discussion about the potential of poetry in higher education but also a practical guide to bring about meaningful change.

The first step towards integrating poetry into higher education teaching practices is to understand it as a method, not a subject. When viewed as such, poetry can be used to facilitate various learning outcomes, be it enhancing the students' understanding of a discipline (Walshe, 2017), improving their critical thinking skills (Huye, 2015), or nurturing their creativity and emotional intelligence (Morris et al, 2005).

A starting point to incorporate poetry into your teaching is by aligning it with your course objectives. Begin by reflecting on what you wish your students to achieve by the end of your course and then consider how poetry might help facilitate these outcomes. A carefully selected poem could be used to introduce a complex concept or issue in your field of study.

For example, imagine that you were teaching an Environmental Pollution module as part of an Environmental Science undergraduate degree and wanted to discuss the impact of wildfires on a wide variety of systems, including the dairy industry. The following poem (which was written by Sam) could be used to introduce recent research, which has found that dairy cows exposed to wildfire smoke produce less milk (Anderson et al, 2022).

Smoky Milk

Summer's drought erupts,
as thirsty soils and
crowded scrubs ignite.
Blistered winds tear
across the sky,
dusting each breath
with heat,
and soot,
and blight.
In hazy fields they wait,
unwary monoliths
of black and white
lying prone beneath
our blazing, tainted sheet.
Lactation lacerated
by the febrile touch

of our distant,
tainted hands.

Students could also be asked to write a poem to consolidate their learning of a topic, thereby encouraging them to think creatively and critically about the subject matter.

Recognising that many students are assessment-driven, it is essential to ensure that the integration of poetry does not feel like a mere add-on, but rather a meaningful and assessed component of the course. This requires strategic planning and sequencing of learning activities. Starting with simple, accessible poems and progressing to more intricate ones can help students acclimatise to poetry. Furthermore, to encourage engagement, it is advisable to align poetry writing activities with key topics of study and make clear their relevance to the course's assessments and overall objectives.

These concepts will be revisited and expanded upon in subsequent sections of the book. However, for now, the presentation of case studies provides a valuable approach to comprehend the practical application and consequential impact of using poetry within the sphere of higher education.

Case study 1.1: Using poetry to teach geography

Key takeaway: Highlights the symbiotic relationship between poetry and geography education, using the sensory language of poetry to deepen understanding of spatial phenomena.

Daniel P. Donaldson (2001) offers an insightful exploration into the symbiotic relationship between poetry and the teaching of geographical principles. Donaldson asserts that poetry, often laden with rich, sensory descriptions of physical and human phenomena spread across space, is an untapped reservoir of illustrative examples for geographic concepts.

This study makes use of William Pattison's four traditions of geography (spatial, area studies, human-land, earth science) as a foundation to underline how these concepts might also be observed in selected poetry. In doing so, Donaldson marries geographical learning with the works of literary luminaries like Walt Whitman, Robert Frost, and Maya Angelou.

Central to the study is the emphasis on the geographic cornerstone of comprehending the unique characteristics of places. Poetry, it suggests, can help learners grasp spatial phenomena from a qualitative lens, venturing beyond the traditional confines of empirical learning. For instance, poems can encapsulate narratives around the human costs associated with securing and maintaining global resources or illustrate the vulnerability of humankind against climatic elements.

Further, Donaldson offers actionable guidance on implementing poetry within geography classrooms. Students, he proposes, could use the oeuvre of renowned poets known for their focus on physical or human processes. They could then choose a specific poem, dissect its thematic content, and develop a brief presentation on how the chosen piece enhances understanding of the human or physical geography at a given location.

Beyond the simple act of using poetry as a reportage or illustrative tool to explore the uniqueness of places, Donaldson encourages learners to generate their own verses. This practice aids students in fostering a profound, qualitative appreciation of spatial phenomena.

Donaldson's study concludes by underlining the potency of poetry as an instrumental asset in geography education. He posits that the abstract and context-rich language employed by poets can offer deeper insights into our understanding of the world and its inhabitants. This methodology enhances the benefits of reading popular poetry and represents a potent addition to teaching and learning about our global community.

Case study 1.2: Poetry and management education

Key takeaway: This study explores how poetry can convey management principles, offering a qualitative depth to learning that complements traditional teaching methods.

In their 2022 study, Matilda Dahl et al explore the potential of poetry as a conduit for delivering management education. Their work emerges from a pedagogical experiment incorporated into a master's in Sustainable

Management in Sweden, wherein the scholars fostered a poetic approach to the teaching and learning process.

The authors critically examine the current approach to management education, which is often narrowly focused on results and efficiency. This focus can overlook the important roles of creativity, critical thinking, and emotional connection. To counteract this, they propose a 'poetic teaching space', an idea inspired by French philosopher Gaston Bachelard. This space encourages students to slow down, reflect, connect emotionally, and engage more deeply with what they are learning.

They make use of several innovative teaching methods during their study. For example, students were asked to observe animals and write poetry based on their observations, helping them build a deeper connection with nature. The authors also conducted a 'non-digital experiment', where they removed all digital devices from the classroom. This encouraged students to focus more intensely on their learning and created a more engaging classroom environment.

Reflecting on the study, the authors suggest that this poetic teaching space helped students understand management principles on a deeper and more qualitative level. They argue that this approach can complement traditional teaching methods in management education, creating a more comprehensive, engaging, and emotionally resonant learning experience.

This case study puts forward a strong argument for integrating poetry and a more personal, qualitative teaching approach into higher education. It shows how fostering emotional engagement with learning can improve the quality of education, making it more impactful and meaningful for students.

Case study 1.3: Poetry in nursing education

Key takeaway: Explores the impact of poetry on developing moral sensitivity among nurses, showing that ethical care extends beyond knowledge to encompass self-awareness and empathy.

Rashidi et al (2022) explore the potential of poetry to impact on the moral sensitivity of nurses in the context of ethics education. When providing care to others, nurses must be able to understand complex ethical issues and make sound decisions which comply with their professional codes. Such understanding moves beyond the cognitive realm and nurses need to develop high levels of self-awareness and self-monitoring, to support their decision making, often in difficult situations.

The authors critically examine current approaches to ethics education, which might place a greater focus on the cognitive than the emotional aspects of learning. Their intervention involves the provision of published poems alongside booklets incorporating ethical principles, to consolidate learning in this area. The poems written by poets such as Jalāl al-Dīn Muḥammad Rūmī (Rumi), cover themes compatible with nursing professional ethics. The effect of this intervention was a longer lasting change in the moral sensitivity of nurses, compared to those who received the booklets on ethical principles alone.

This study suggests the wording, rhythm, and language of poetry is central to the memory and recollection of ethical concepts. By choosing memorable poems, nurses were found to remember more over a longer period, with this approach also positively affecting self-awareness development and knowledge of the ethical principles.

This study puts forward a strong case for integrating poetry in ethics education, an important aspect of professional development for nurses. More generally, this work shows that poetry provides a way to connect with the emotions to improve the quality of education and make it longer lasting than other more traditional methods of learning.

The future of poetry in higher education

Poetry has the potential to create a transformative educational experience that is at once more human, more personal, and more meaningful. As we move forward, we see an educational landscape that values this contribution, giving poetry its rightful place as a respected pedagogical tool across various disciplines.

Poetry holds the potential to counterbalance the often cold, calculated world of data that higher education can sometimes become. As a medium that touches the heart as much as it stimulates the mind, poetry encourages the holistic development of students, fostering emotional intelligence, empathy, creativity, and critical thinking.

Moreover, the use of poetry in higher education will be bolstered by advancements in technology. Digital platforms can facilitate the sharing and discussion of poems, and online learning environments offer new opportunities for integrating poetry in teaching. For instance, the use of virtual or augmented reality technology could allow students to experience poetry in entirely novel ways, such as visualising the metaphorical landscapes of poems or exploring a poem's structure in three dimensions (Wild et al, 2021).

However, the journey ahead is not without challenges. While we are optimistic about the potential of poetry in higher education, we recognise the difficulties involved in bringing about this change. Resistance from some corners of the educational community is to be expected. Nonetheless, we are confident that the compelling arguments and practical strategies presented in this book, coupled with the shared commitment and passion of educators like you, the reader, can make a significant impact.

Further study

The 'Further study' sections that you will find in each chapter of this book are designed to guide your independent exploration, stimulating your curiosity and offering avenues for deeper understanding and broader engagement.

Look to the research. Take time to review the references listed at the end of the book. Choose two or three studies that provide insights into integrating poetry in higher education contexts like yours. Carefully analyse how their evidence and examples support the use of poetry within your academic discipline. Make detailed notes on the key takeaways from those references that are most applicable to enhancing your own teaching through poetry. Consulting this substantive research will substantiate the value of incorporating poetry into your own pedagogical practice.

Immerse yourself in poetry archives. Explore online poetry archives such as The Poetry Foundation, The Academy of American Poets, and The Poetry Archive. Spend time reading widely to find two or three poems that resonate with your academic discipline, whether through relevant themes, emotions evoked, or ideas explored. Engage with the selected poems by reading them aloud and reflecting on what they evoke within you. Consider how these poems could inspire or intellectually challenge both you and your students, and how the poems could potentially illuminate or add depth to topics or themes within your field.

Start to weave poetry into your teaching. Record your thoughts and reflections on the specific connections you see between the poems you have selected from the archives and your own teaching context. Brainstorm practical, concrete ways those poems could complement and enhance your instructional approach. Outline tentative plans for how you might integrate the poems into actual lessons, classroom activities, assignments, or assessments. Then, add these poems into your educational toolkit to draw on as needed to organically enrich your students' learning experiences. This might seem like too much of a stretch at this point in your pedagogic poetic development, but we will be exploring exactly how to do so throughout the remainder of this book.

Summary

In Chapter 1, we have explored the current landscape of higher education, a system that is often characterised by speed, performativity, and standardisation. We discussed how these characteristics, while significant, can potentially overshadow the importance of creativity, individuality, and diversity in learning approaches.

We made a case for the role of poetry, highlighting its potential benefits within the context of higher education. By discussing its history and status in education, backed by relevant literature and studies, we also started to demonstrate the compelling connection between poetry and transformative learning.

Recognising the possible challenges faced by educators, we broached the topic of resistance within the higher education community and the dearth of resources. To fully realise the potential of poetry as a tool in higher education it is important to face these challenges head on.

Diverse case studies and practical strategies have also been offered, demonstrating the impact of using poetry and its versatility across disciplines. We will build on these examples throughout the rest of the book. Our aim is to inspire educators to adopt similar practices in their classrooms, contributing to a more engaging, empathic, and creative learning environment.

Finally, we looked towards the future of poetry in higher education. We encouraged you to consider your role in this evolving landscape and to begin to explore integrating poetry into your own teaching practice. By doing so, we hope to instil a sense of agency, empowerment, and optimism about the journey ahead.

Now, as we move into Chapter 2, we are going to investigate the 'how' of using poetry in our teaching practices. We will provide an expanded range of examples and case studies, illustrating the versatile ways in which poetry can be woven into various teaching contexts. We will explore the ways in which poetry can be harnessed as an instructional tool to foster critical thinking and empathy among students – competencies that are imperative in our swiftly evolving society. The stage is now set to explore and unleash the transformative potential of poetry in your own educational environments.

TWO

Using poetry in the classroom

Chapter highlights

- Exploring the practical use of poetry in teaching environments.
- The role of poetry in enhancing critical thinking, creativity, and engagement.
- Strategies for facilitating poetry sessions and addressing challenges.
- Case studies and examples of poetry integration across different disciplines.
- Emphasis on timing, authenticity, and 'good enough' poetry in teaching.

Introduction

The aim of this chapter is to explore the intricacies of using poetry in teaching, considering the ways in which we can use both published and student-authored poems in our educational endeavours. There will be an expanded range of examples covering several subject areas, and case studies, to bring the concepts to life in ways which we hope will be helpful for your practice. We will also explore potential challenges to using poetry in teaching, to prepare you to manage common situations which might arise when working creatively.

Poetry can make learning and teaching more interactive and engaging than other traditionally used methods, which is helpful for learners to develop skills of critical thinking, analysis, synthesis, and creativity. However, alongside such development can come a more unpredictable learning environment, as we never know exactly how a poem will be interpreted by a learner or similarly, how they might respond to a creative writing task.

Educators need to be open to vulnerability, both with learners and themselves. As such, we will consider how poetry can foster authenticity in teaching, helping to create connections and spark change for both teachers and students. We will also explore the practicalities of facilitation including decisions relating to the type of task, preparation, and strategies for managing large groups and fostering peer learning with poetry.

The versatility of poetry in teaching

Poetry offers versatility in teaching practice and there are several ways it has been used previously to support a range of learners and disciplines. For example, published poetry can be adopted to develop paraphrase skills with international law students (Nilon, 2020), or law educators might write their own poems, to help scaffold a bespoke educational purpose (Manley, 2018). In nursing education, students can be supported to write poetry to develop their writing confidence and reflective skills (Cronin and Hawthorne, 2019), read published poetry to relieve stress (Park et al, 2022), or develop empathy towards others (Mood, 2018).

Poetry has been helpfully used to support professional development in teacher education (Jawaheer, 2023) and building on the medical humanities movement, Quinlan (2021) proposes an 'educational humanities', to support the development of the relational, emotional, and ethical concerns of developing teachers. The value of the medical humanities movement is well documented in the teaching of medical students; for example, to promote reflection, analyse care provision, understand the patient perspective, support communication skills, and develop empathy (Kumagai, 2014, 2017; Cole et al, 2015; Joshi et al, 2022).

It is clear through this selection of examples that poetry can be used in different settings, with a wide range of aims, enabling us to view our practice through a different lens. The discussion here is not exhaustive and if you cannot see your specific area of expertise, do not let that put you off. As this chapter unfolds you will see how the techniques and methods are applicable on a wider scale, as poetry has an ability to support all learners in deeper and more imaginative learning, whatever the speciality.

Before you start

When introducing poetry in your teaching practice, there are some practicalities that might be helpful to explore before you start. Planning, such as timing of sessions, group size, and type of activity are aspects which are helpful to get right at the beginning to promote later success. Introducing poetry into your teaching can lead to exciting although unpredictable outcomes, therefore planning as much as you can in advance is recommended. For example, how will you deal with resistance from students who might not believe that engagement with poetry is a good use of their time, when what they signed up for was, for example, a course about business?

At the start of her creative teaching journey, Kirsten remembers enthusiastically announcing to her first-year undergraduate nursing group of 150 students that she would be introducing poetry writing to consider nursing knowledge, skills, and experiences in a more innovative and interesting way. This was immediately met with a loud comment from a male student on the front row, "I want to be a nurse, not a ruddy poet!" It can be easy to be put off balance by such comments, especially when we are inexperienced and not sure of either ourselves or our new techniques and at that time, Kirsten did not have an answer.

However, what she learned from this experience was to be more confident in the use of poetry to support learning. While poetry is not for everyone, it can offer transformative experiences for some students. Although certain learners may prefer more structured teaching styles and find unpredictability unsettling, engaging with poetry still broadens their horizons. At the very least, they will learn to appreciate other perspectives, even if they are hesitant to share their own.

An advantage of poetry is that it provides a way to support learners to engage more authentically with the subject areas, themselves, and other students in the group. Poetry sessions, whether they involve published poems or are student-authored, can be more variable, leading to in-depth learning which taps into the emotions in ways that other methods might not. For some, this might be overwhelming and lead to some learners feeling upset, sad, or tearful.

Rather than avoid engaging with poetry altogether, we agree with Pennebaker and Evans (2014) who suggest this rarely happens when asking learners to write expressively. Even if it does, this is not necessarily a bad thing and often, learners are pleased to have an opportunity to discuss emotionally challenging events or topics with supportive others, with whom they can find connection. Indeed, there are opportunities for the rehearsal of empathy within a group, when learners listen to the perspectives of others, and begin to understand how they might differ from their own.

However, we do suggest learners avoid topics that they might feel are too overwhelming to discuss in a classroom situation. The classroom is not a space for counselling or therapy, and to help ensure this, we recommend employing the effective 'flip out' rule of Pennebaker and Evans (2014). This rule can be introduced at the beginning of any poetry sessions. It essentially means that if a learner encounters a topic that feels too upsetting or intense to discuss at that moment, they should 'flip out' of that topic, setting it to one side. They can then choose to revisit it later when they feel more prepared to handle it. This approach allows learners to manage their emotional wellbeing while engaging with potentially sensitive material. Learners can also be directed to supportive services within the setting, such as counselling, should this be required.

A path to authenticity

Having discussed what might happen should a learner become upset, there is another question when working with poetry in the classroom, be that published, or learner/facilitator authored. This concerns our actions if *we* get upset by what we read or hear. Poetry is powerful and both Kirsten and Sam can cite several examples when they have become tearful in the classroom, on hearing poetry shared by learners, or when using published poems as a springboard from which to discuss topics.

However, if we want to connect with students in a meaningful way, sharing in the learning process is important and this is especially so with creative work, when learners might feel particularly exposed or vulnerable (Cranton, 2016). Learning more about ourselves through poetry is not restricted to our students and is something with which we can engage as facilitators and educators. We have several different roles in our relationships with learners and it can be difficult to know where the boundaries should lie, especially when considering other aspects of our position; for example, the assessment and grading of student work (Cranton and Carusetta, 2004).

We might not want to share too much, although taking an authentic stance can encourage discourse in the classroom, which is important as it helps students to make sense of who they are and the experiences they have had (Jack and Wibberley, 2014). Further, connecting authentically with students can act as a reminder for us about what it was like to be in their position, thereby engendering empathy, strengthening mutual understanding, and enhancing connection which moves beyond the cognitive realm.

Speaking from a legal education perspective, Marlow (2015) suggests being authentic in our teaching is the first step in humanising what we do, and ultimately gives us more satisfaction in doing so. This might include sharing our own poetry, although as Manley (2018) outlines, even when we recite the work of others, while it might not reflect our own views precisely, it still conveys some authenticity. Of course, we need to feel comfortable sharing our poetry, and the extent to which we disclose something of ourselves through our writing will vary.

For example, writing from a nursing perspective, Kirsten's poetry often explores loss and grief, which she has shared readily with learners in the classroom. This not only conveys authenticity but gives permission to the group to do the same, encouraging the development of self-awareness and honesty. Similarly, Sam's poetry often explores issues surrounding the climate crisis, which is a subject that many students feel strongly about, and which creates opportunities for further discussion, exploration, and shared learning.

Further, such actions promote an egalitarian relationship with the learners, as the leadership starts to be transferred across the group as it becomes more autonomous and self-sustaining (Mezirow, 1997). However, we might feel uncomfortable about sharing our poetry for other reasons, which move beyond the emotional. To what extent can we, as educators, call ourselves poets, and how do we know that our poetry is worth hearing?

'Good enough' poetry

Just like the learners you support; it is up to you to decide how much of yourself and your poetry you are willing to share. This might depend on several factors such as your confidence, your knowledge of the learners, your relationship with them, and how comfortable you are with any potential feelings of vulnerability. You might also worry that the standard of your poetry is not high enough for students to hear.

However, having a fierce inner critic or feeling frightened of perceived failure in front of students can not only block creativity but, with it, opportunities for meaningful communication (Creely et al, 2019). Learners will likely be feeling the same way that you are, and it is common for them to seek reassurance that what they have written is what was required (Majorana and Van Deusen, 2022). Some will feel poetry writing is an intimidating exercise (Manley, 2018) and be quick to judge the quality of their work in negative terms, perhaps describing their writing as inadequate or inferior to that of their peers.

Keeping a level of self-awareness is helpful for you as an educator and facilitator, as when discussing learner contributions, it can be easy to show preference for some work over others. Instead, aim to keep the focus on the process of the poem development, not the final product, as all learners will have a contribution to the discussion, however small. Indeed, even learners who barely engage in poetry writing, will still develop their creativity and skills of analysis by listening to the perspectives brought forward by the writing of others.

Lahman and Richard (2014, p 352) propose the concept of 'good enough' poetry, which recognises a creative space where researchers, regardless of their expertise in writing poems, can initially craft raw and unpolished pieces that have the potential to evolve. In the context of higher education, this concept underlines the importance of the process of engaging with poetry as a tool for learning and reflection, rather than focusing solely on the product (the poem). Embracing all levels of poetic output can enrich the educational experience, recognising that while some work may be more polished, every contribution has value.

EXERCISE 2.1: FURTHERING YOUR RELATIONSHIP WITH POETRY

Estimated engagement time: 2–3 hours.

Aim: To deepen personal engagement with a meaningful poem, reflect on the experience, and apply the insights gained to enhance teaching practices.

Objectives:

- Analyse personal reactions to a meaningful poem.
- Identify potential student experiences in engaging with poetry.
- Discuss teaching goals to support students in developing engaging relationships with poetry.

Output: A one-page reflection on personal engagement with a meaningful poem and a list of teaching goals to facilitate rich poetic encounters for students.

Type of exercise: Individual.

Materials needed:

- Writing materials (pen and paper or digital device).
- The poem chosen for reflection.

Activity:

Step 1: Revisit a meaningful poem

Take time to re-read and reflect on a poem you previously connected with in a meaningful way (for example one that you identified in Exercise 1.1). Carefully consider what originally drew you to this work. Was it the theme, writing style, perspective or emotional resonance that compelled you? Make notes on the specific elements that sparked your interest.

Step 2: Analyse your reaction

Consider the nature of your personal reaction and relationship to the poem. Does it speak to you on an emotional level? Does it evoke certain memories or transport you to a particular time or place? Does it offer you an insightful perspective? Make detailed notes unpacking the nuances of how this poem resonates with you.

Step 3: Explore the resonance

Expand your reflection into a one-page written piece exploring exactly what it is about this poem that resonates so deeply with you. Dig deeper into the specific aspects that hold personal meaning and why they affect you. Articulate the deeper connections this work sparks for you.

Step 4: Empathise with students' experiences

Considering your own meaningful poetic encounter, empathise with the learning journey students may have as they explore impactful poems.

Appreciate how poetry can elicit powerful responses from learners as well.

Step 5: Apply insights to teaching

Use the insights from your reflection to thoughtfully consider how you can best support students in developing their own engaging relationships with poetry. Set specific goals for your teaching practice focused on facilitating rich, memorable poetic encounters that foster appreciation and understanding.

Having explored how we might relate to poetry in the context of our authentic being when connecting with learners, we will now move on to more practical matters in terms of how to implement both poetry reading and creative writing into your classroom teaching, beginning with the importance of timing.

Timing

Introducing poetry into curricula can be unexpected for learners, sometimes perceived as less serious or even intimidating. To mitigate this and aid in its successful integration, careful timing and relation to other curriculum aspects are important. Scaffolding, a key educational strategy, involves building a supportive structure for learning. It starts with basic concepts and gradually moves towards more complex ideas. This method helps students connect new ideas like poetry to their existing knowledge, making the learning process more approachable and effective. Scaffolding ensures that students are not overwhelmed and can progressively build their understanding and appreciation of poetry in a structured and supportive way.

Majorana and Van Deusen (2022) incorporate poetry into their teaching from the very first session, using it as a tool for students to introduce themselves and foster a sense of community in the learning environment. They encourage students to create an autobiographical poem following a specific structure as a means of self-expression and to initiate the building

Table 2.1: Template for creating an autobiographical poem

Line number	Description
1	Your First Name
2	A colour that describes you
3	A significant community in your life
4	Three places or experiences you cherish
5	Three aspirations or dreams
6	Three accomplishments you are proud of
7	Three lessons you have learned in life
8	Your favourite hobbies or interests
9	What you think of poetry
10	Your Last Name

of a learning community. This approach allows students to share aspects of their identity and experiences creatively.

To assist you in introducing this creative exercise to your students, Table 2.1 offers a structured template for composing an autobiographical poem. This structure is designed to be flexible, so feel free to adapt it to better suit the needs and experiences of your learners. Such poems can be developed in both length and style, to include topics of your choice and can also enable you to gain understanding about students' hopes, fears, and expectations. Following this structure, here is an illustrative example to show how it can be brought to life:

> Aisha
> Azure, like a calm ocean
> Part of a close-knit book club
> Strolling through lavender fields, first snowfall, nights under the stars
> Wants to publish a novel, travel the Silk Road, learn pottery
> Built a car, is fluent in French, ran a marathon
> Kindness wins, listen more, every failure is a lesson

Reads mysteries, paints landscapes, bakes on Sundays
Is apprehensive but excited
Patel

Modelling the process by writing your own autobiographical poem, can enable you to connect with your learners by sharing something of yourself from the outset and laying out your expectations in a way that connects with others, rather than a more didactic approach. Introducing poetry activities early in the curricula also secures a place for such activities right from the start and establishes them as part of the norm of what we do. Further, planning sessions so that they do not coincide with busy times; for example, heavy assessment periods, assists learners to engage more creatively and enables them to gain the most benefit from these encounters.

Where to start

When introducing poetry into your repertoire, it can be helpful to start by exploring a poem, which might relate to the subject area you are teaching or more simply, to start thinking about the wider discipline. Writing from a business education context, Morgan et al (2010) used an introductory poem which concerns what poetry expects from us. The poem 'Introduction to Poetry', by Billy Collins (1996), an American poet noted for his humorous observations on life, was used to explore the different ways we can read and interpret poems. The poem creatively illustrates various ways we can approach and interpret poetry, encouraging readers to explore it in a more open and less analytical manner. Collins humorously contrasts this exploratory approach with a common tendency to scrutinise poetry intensely to extract its meaning. His work serves as an accessible entry point for those new or hesitant about engaging with poetry.

Starting conversations about poetry in this way can be helpful to explore how poetry is open to interpretation by the reader, reassuring learners there are no wrong answers, just differences in the way we might understand things. Exercise 2.2 provides an example that you might wish to try with your learners, outlining one of the ways in which you might read (and discuss) a poem.

EXERCISE 2.2: READ A POEM

Estimated engagement time: 90–120 minutes.

Aim: To engage students in reading, discussing, and reflecting on poetry, enhancing their understanding and appreciation of poetic language and themes.

Objectives:

- Introduce students to the process of reading and interpreting poetry.
- Engage students in discussing imagery, themes, and personal resonance found in different poems.
- Adopt an appreciation for the depth and diversity of interpretation that poetry offers.

Output: Group and individual reflections on the poems read and discussed, as well as a broader understanding and appreciation of engaging with poetry.

Type of exercise: Group and individual.

Materials needed:

- Copies of selected poems.
- Writing materials (pen and paper or digital device) for taking notes and writing reflections.

Activity:

Step 1: Introduction to poem reading

Briefly introduce the idea of reading a poem, explaining that unlike prose, poetry often relies on imagery, rhythm, and a compact use of language to convey its message. Mention that there is no single 'right' way to interpret a poem, but rather in doing so we bring all our own individual lives and lived experiences to the process.

Step 2: Select a poem

Choose a poem related to your taught material or one that encapsulates a universal theme. Distribute copies of the poem to the students.

Step 3: Silent reading

Allow students a few minutes to read the poem silently, encouraging them to notice any initial reactions, emotions, or images that come to mind.

Step 4: Read aloud

Read the poem aloud to the class or invite a volunteer to do so. Discuss how hearing the poem might have altered or deepened their understanding.

Step 5: Vocabulary check

Identify and discuss any unfamiliar words or phrases. Explore the meanings and how they contribute to the poem's overall effect.

Step 6: Imagery and theme discussion

Divide students into small groups to discuss the imagery and themes of the poem. Encourage them to share different interpretations and support their ideas with lines from the poem.

Step 7: Share insights

Reconvene as a class and have a representative from each group share their insights. Discuss the various interpretations and how the language of the poem supports them.

Step 8: Personal reflection

Ask students to write a brief reflection on how the poem resonated with them personally, and what new understanding or appreciation they gained through this exercise.

Step 9: Repeat with new poems

Repeat Steps 2–8 with a couple of different poems to provide more practice in reading and discussing poetry, and to expose students to a variety of poetic styles and themes.

Step 10: Wrap-up discussion

Conclude with a discussion on how this exercise has perhaps altered your learners' approach to reading poetry and how the skills learned might be applied to other areas of study or life.

There are other ways to encourage creativity. For example, identifying a favourite catchy song can be helpful for learners to establish a rhythm, from which they can add words to begin their poem. They can keep the melody and rhythm of the song but remove the original words, substituting them for their own creative thoughts.

For others, writing lists of words and phrases associated with the topic they want to write about can be helpful as a starting point. They can then frame their poem around these important words. Encouraging students to write, in the moment, without any expectation of the outcome, removes the pressure to 'write a poem' and can lead to a freedom rarely found in academic writing. Exercise 2.3 provides a structure for how you might do this in your own practice.

EXERCISE 2.3: WRITE A LIST POEM

Estimated engagement time: 30–45 minutes.

Aim: To engage students in creative thinking and expression through the construction of list poems related to class material.

Objectives:

- Introduce students to the concept of list poems.
- Adopt creative thinking and expression related to specified or chosen topics.
- Discuss sharing and discussion of creative work to explore different perspectives and ideas.

Output: List poems written by students on selected topics and a discussion reflecting on the exercise.

Type of exercise: Individual and group.

Materials needed:

- Writing materials (pen and paper or digital device).
- Timer.

Activity:

Step 1: Explain list poems

Briefly explain what a list poem is – a poem that expresses ideas as a list. Feel free to provide some of your own examples.

Step 2: Choose a topic

Pick a topic related to your taught subject. Tell students they will write a list poem on this topic. You might even collaboratively decide on a topic.

Step 3: Set a timer

Set a timer for 60–90 seconds. Students will write a list poem during this time.

Step 4: Write the list

Instruct students to write down anything related to the topic – words, phrases, images, memories, smells, thoughts. Stress they should write continuously for the whole time. They can write lists of words or whole sentences. There is no strict limit to the form, just encourage them to keep writing until you say stop.

Step 5: Share poems

Have students voluntarily share their list poems. Emphasise that this is a safe space, and that need only share if they feel comfortable in doing so.

Step 6: Repeat with new topics

Repeat Steps 3–5 for two more topics.

Step 7: Discussion

Discuss how the exercise helped students generate ideas. Have them identify lines to use in future poems.

Another way to begin any poetry sessions is to invite leaners to close their eyes and remember the event or topic they want to explore. Ask them to think about the associated thoughts, emotions, colours, and words. Giving time to remember important aspects of an event can then trigger creative writing.

We now continue this chapter by presenting a series of case studies, exploring how educators have used poetry in the classroom, so you can see how it looks in action. In doing so, you will be better equipped with ideas for your own practice and how you might use them in the context of your own teaching.

Case study 2.1: Poetry in law education

Key takeaway: This case study illustrates the versatility of poetry to enhance the teaching of complex subjects like law, showing that creativity can be a key asset in any academic field.

In this study, Stewart Manley (2018) explores 'home-made' poetry to supplement the teaching of trust law. Manley uses narrative poems, written by himself or students, in two universities in Malaysia, where he taught both law and business, using poetry with both groups. Manley discusses the benefits of using poetry in teaching across any academic field and makes the point that the limits of using poetry are only set by the extent of the imagination of both writer and reader.

Manley highlights three main benefits of using poetry in higher education, starting with the way in which it can capture complex concepts and make them easier to understand and remember. This change in medium, from law cases and statutes, which might be dry in nature, to poetry, with its imagery, metaphor, and freedom, requires students to reformulate their thinking about the original concept.

Second, Manley describes how poetry humanises concepts often taught without context, which is the aspect that makes them most important. Poetry has a way to humanise the abstract, and in doing so makes it more memorable and easier to understand. Poetry moves students away from the technical and reminds them of the underpinning purpose and objective of what they are learning.

Lastly, Manley makes the point discussed earlier in this chapter, which relates to the use of poetry in making our teaching more authentic. He shares his own poetry with the group and provides an example of writing which addresses his own personal feelings about how wealthy people might use law loopholes to avoid paying debts.

Manley acknowledges how some students are reluctant to write poetry and that his attempts have been met with mixed success. He uses examples to encourage the students, although his learners report how they found poetry writing an intimidating activity. Rather than ask students to write a poem in the classroom, Manley gives time for them to write their poem at home, which reduces the pressure and leads to more engagement. He makes the point that subjects such as law are heavily biased towards logic, which might explain student reluctance. However, the concepts are often difficult to understand, and poetry can provide opportunities to make challenging ideas more memorable and easier to comprehend.

Manley's ideas offer practical ways to supplement teaching using poetry written by either teachers or students. He suggests that even with a topic as 'dry' as trust law, engaging poetry can be written quite easily. As he points out, there is no database of poetry that will meet all our teaching needs, so we often need to create our own. However, doing so is advantageous in that the educator understands precisely what they want to convey to learners, so can construct something bespoke in contrast to a previously published poem, which might not quite capture the topic that is being discussed.

Case study 2.2: Poetry writing in problem-based learning

Key takeaway: Demonstrates the use of poetry to foster collaborative skills in nursing students, highlighting how creative expression can support problem-solving and learning.

Zenobia C.Y. Chan (2017) combined a patient case study with poetry writing, to promote the collaborative skills of first-year nursing students. During the problem-based learning class, students were given 1 hour to develop a group poem based on a given scenario and subsequently asked to present this to their peers, along with a reflective piece outlining what they had learned. Some learners used metaphors such as the 'devil' and 'angel' to represent unhealthy and healthy lifestyles, developing their poetry into roleplay with a presenter, devil, angel, and patient each playing a part in the story.

All students, even those having no previous experience in poetry writing, found the task straightforward, as they were not trying to produce poems with any artistic value, but were doing so as a learning activity through which poetry was the method rather than the outcome. The learners found no direct relationship between poetry and nursing care, although they stated several learning benefits such as dealing with stress, developing effective presentations, improving cooperation with others, and harnessing their creativity. Further, and perhaps most importantly, they found the activity to be a fun and positive experience.

Case study 2.3: Blackout poetry

Key takeaway: Engaging with blackout poetry can enhance student engagement and analytical skills by creatively interacting with existing texts.

Blackout poetry is a form of found poetry, which involves taking an existing text, for example a newspaper article, and crossing out unrequired words to create a new poem on a particular theme (Ladenheim, 2014). By this method, learners actively craft new poems using their chosen words, enhancing their knowledge development. This technique not only boosts student engagement with challenging topics but also hones their analysis and synthesis skills, which is useful in other study areas. (Ladenheim, 2014).

In 2022, Miguel Gomez used poetry to immerse students in the voices of marginalised historical figures, encouraging critical thinking about their importance. Gomez sourced concise extracts from speeches, online materials, and diaries, with a focus on often-overlooked voices. Students analysed these insights and crafted blackout poetry, highlighting words or phrases that resonated with them, then using a marker to black out the remaining text, formed a poem from the chosen words. Afterwards, students shared and discussed their creations, exploring the interesting facets of each other's work.

This activity was found to enable students to develop new understanding of both marginalised voices from history and the way in which we engage with and interpret primary sources. Discussions that followed the creation of the poetry were also found to develop critical thinking, as students rationalised both their word selections and omissions.

EXERCISE 2.4: SKETCHING YOUR POETIC APPROACH

Estimated engagement time: Variable, depending on depth of planning (recommend allocating at least 1–2 hours).

Aim: To develop a personalised poetry teaching strategy tailored to address discipline-specific challenges and engage learners effectively.

Objective:

- Analyse identified discipline-specific challenges.
- Identify relevant case studies of poetry use in higher education.
- Draft an actionable strategy for integrating chosen poetry approaches into instruction.

Outputs: A detailed strategy outline for integrating poetry into teaching, including lesson plans, activities, and assessments.

Type of exercise: Individual.

Materials needed:

- Access to case studies and other relevant literature.
- Writing materials (pen and paper or digital device).

Activity:

Step 1: Revisit discipline-specific challenges

Return to the two or three challenging aspects of your discipline you identified in Exercise 1.2. Re-familiarise yourself with these topics or concepts.

Step 2: Analyse case studies

Carefully analyse three or four case studies that used poetry in similar higher education contexts (starting with those discussed previously). Identify techniques relevant to your needs, like composing original poems or analysing existing works.

Step 3: Select appropriate approaches

Choose one or two approaches that align with your discipline-specific challenges and teaching objectives. Consider adaptations needed to optimise suitability. You might draw inspiration from Manley's (2018) work, by taking a line from one of these aspects and writing your own poem. Alternatively, you could adopt an approach like that of Chan (2017) which requires students to write group poems, based on information you provide. Or you might like to use existing texts, such as important speeches, as discussed by Gómez (2022), to enable your learners to analyse and synthesise information in a creative way.

Step 4: Outline your strategy

Outline a strategy for integrating the selected approaches into your instruction. Include practical details like lesson plans, activities, assessments (see Chapter 3), and additional resources. Chapter 2 provides some specific advice for how you might do this.

Step 5: Refine for student needs

Consider your student population and refine aspects of the strategy to best engage them. Incorporate sufficient scaffolding, tailored to your learners. You might want to begin by revisiting the two or three aspects you identified in Step 1 of this exercise as this will determine your approach.

Addressing challenges and finding solutions

Through the case studies presented in this chapter, we have explored ways in which poetry can be used in various higher education settings. Choosing a suitable approach will be dependent on learning outcomes, your knowledge of the group, and your own confidence in trying something new. However, we must acknowledge that our pedagogical choices might be influenced by other factors, which might prove challenging, such as room availability, time, and whether we need to enlist other colleagues to support our efforts.

Healy and Smyth (2017) reflect on their use of poetry with a group of 40 general and intellectual disability nursing students, to explore attitudes to ageing in a lecture context. Following a whole group discussion about their attitudes to ageing, a poem was recited to the students titled 'An Old Lady', more commonly known as 'What do you see nurse?' (an anonymous poem found in a bedside locker of an older woman, after her death). Following this recital, learners worked in groups of three to discuss their perceptions of caring for older people and any important issues that need to be considered. Learning in this way supported critical and creative thinking in the group and enabled the educator to share their own experiences of working with older people. Incorporating poetry within a lecture format supports student engagement by providing education on two levels: enabling a mix of didactic learning and collaborative experience.

Other ways to manage larger groups of students might involve making use of digital tools. For example, Google Meet was shown to be an effective way to enable the development of social and collaborative skills via the sharing of student authored poems, although the usual connectivity problems can prevail (Acim, 2023). Similarly, X (née Twitter) has been demonstrated as an effective place for learners and educators to share their poetry, creating greater opportunities for feedback and collaboration (Januchowski-Hartley et al, 2018).

Managing larger groups of students is also an excellent opportunity to involve colleagues in your use of poetry as a teaching method. Doing so can enable more in-depth discussion, which often arises when students are faced with poetry which questions their previously held assumptions and can also help to demonstrate the benefit of such an approach. However, enlisting colleagues can be challenging especially when they might be sceptical or uncomfortable using poetry in this way.

As discussed by Morgan et al (2010), poetry can be destabilising, challenging, and has the potential to move us away from the safety of a set of slides we might have been teaching with for years. Just like our students, we need to prepare our colleagues, and this could start with introductory poetry exercises like those described in the section 'Where to start'. Our experience of using poetry in teaching has shown us that often there will be a few like-minded colleagues in your area who are keen to try new methods. Alternatively, you can engage in cross departmental teaching, inviting poetry academics into your subject world to model collaborative working and enrich creativity in your classroom.

EXERCISE 2.5: PREPARING FOR LAUNCH

Estimated engagement time: Variable, depending on the depth of planning and engagement with colleagues (we recommend allocating at least 2–4 hours).

Aim: To prepare adequately for the integration of poetry-based teaching in your practice, and to engage colleagues and students for a smooth, impactful launch.

Objectives:

- Identify potential challenges and devise mitigation strategies.
- Analyse the perspectives of supportive colleagues.
- Conduct a preparatory workshop to experience poetry-based activities.

Output: A comprehensive preparation plan including identified challenges, mitigation strategies, engaged colleagues, workshop design, and defined personal boundaries.

Type of exercise: Individual (Steps 1, 2, and 5); group (Steps 3 and 4).

Materials needed:

- Writing materials (pen and paper or digital device).
- Venue and resources for a preparation workshop (if applicable).

Activity:

Step 1: Identify potential challenges

Reflect on two or three reasonable challenges that could arise when integrating poetry into your teaching based on your specific context. These may relate to student reluctance to engage, disruption of classroom norms, or increased preparation requirements. Carefully list each anticipated challenge and describe why it poses a credible issue you may need to mitigate.

Step 2: Develop mitigation strategies

For each of the challenges you identified, develop one or two tangible action steps you can take to effectively manage or overcome the issue should it arise. For example, you may plan to scaffold poetry writing techniques if students struggle or conduct check-ins after introducing poetic discussions to gauge engagement. Detail the strategy for each challenge.

Step 3: Engage colleagues thoughtfully

Consider which one or two colleagues could serve as strong allies or supports as you embark on using poetry in your teaching. Develop a clear, thoughtful plan for introducing them to the concept, such as sharing a powerful poem as a discussion catalyst. Outline how you will explain your goals and gather their perspectives.

Step 4: Run a preparation workshop

Design and facilitate a poetry teaching preparation workshop for engaged colleagues and invite additional department members. Guide them through sample poetry-based activities to experience the approach first-hand. Gather their feedback to refine strategies to optimise student engagement and learning.

Step 5: Define personal boundaries

Take time to deeply reflect on your personal boundaries regarding sharing emotions or experiences prompted by poetry in the classroom. Determine specifically what types of reflections or stories you are comfortable disclosing versus keeping private to maintain professionalism. Articulate these boundaries clearly to guide your real-time teaching choices.

Further study

Expanding your skills in effectively leveraging poetry for pedagogy requires dedicated exploration. The following activities are designed to deepen your understanding of applying poetic techniques and finding inspiration from others.

Analyse pedagogical poetry techniques. Revisit the case studies from Chapter 1 and Chapter 2 and identify two or three specific poetry techniques that seem particularly relevant for your teaching context, such as having students author original poems or using found poetry. Consider how implementing these techniques in your classroom could meaningfully support your learning outcomes and develop required competencies in your learners. Make detailed notes outlining your thoughts on how you might adapt and apply these techniques, considering the resources, student needs, and time investment required to optimise their impact.

Gather peer feedback. Develop a draft lesson plan that details how you would apply one of the identified poetry techniques in your own practice. Be sure to articulate clear learning outcomes, choose appropriate poetry content, map out a timeline, and delineate in-class tasks and exercises. Share this draft lesson plan with some trusted colleagues and gather their feedback on its feasibility, suggestions for how it could be strengthened or refined, and their perceptions of the potential benefits it could provide students. Use these valuable peer insights to iterate and improve your lesson plan until you feel it is well-designed for successfully bringing poetry into your praxis.

Immerse yourself in inspiring examples. Look through the references at the end of this book, and curate a couple of examples from these resources that you find particularly inspiring in their approach and content. Reflect on how these examples might translate to your context or spark ideas for novel applications of poetry. Also consider what would need to be modified to better suit your own practice and learners.

Summary

Chapter 2 has explored how poetry can be used to bring new and different perspectives to subjects and support us to keep our teaching interesting, engaging, and fun. We have seen how poetry can enable students to develop skills of analysis, synthesis, personal, and professional development enabling a deeper understanding of not only the topics under discussion but also of themselves.

We have explored the different ways poetry can be used in the classroom, using examples which involve published poetry, or artistic expressions developed in a bespoke way by educators, to meet the needs of their learners. We have shown how poetry can be used alongside other well-known pedagogic methods such as problem-based learning, from which students can write their own poetry. Practical methods, such as blackout poetry serve as a sound starting point for learners to develop their own priorities when it comes to deciding what is important in their understanding.

We now progress into Chapter 3, where we will explore how we can use poetry as a tool to create innovative and authentic ways to support our assessment and feedback practices.

THREE

Poetry as assessment

Chapter highlights

- Poetry's role in authentic assessment in education.
- Designing poetry-based assessments for various learning outcomes.
- Addressing challenges and barriers in using poetry for assessment and feedback.
- Case studies illustrating the use of poetry in assessing student understanding.

Introduction

Assessment is a pivotal component of the learning process in higher education. Well-designed assessments allow educators to gauge students' understanding, provide meaningful feedback, and empower students to apply their knowledge in authentic contexts (Mueller, 2005). However, traditional forms of assessment like exams and essays often fall short of these goals, typically testing rote memorisation rather than deeper learning. This chapter explores how poetry can reinvigorate assessment, serving as a creative, engaging, and insightful alternative to conventional tests.

Poetry offers several advantages when employed as an assessment technique in both formative and summative assessments. Firstly, it necessitates that students synthesise and connect ideas rather than simply regurgitate facts (Wardle and Illingworth, 2022). The constraints of the poetic form compel students to be selective yet meaningful with language, distilling concepts down to their essence. This promotes the type of cognitive engagement that transforms surface-level learning into deeper, lasting comprehension (Brown, 2019).

Additionally, poetry provides an avenue for learners to connect academic concepts to their own unique contexts, cultures, and experiences. By incorporating their voices into the assessment process, students feel empowered and invested in their education (Nguyen-Truong et al, 2018). This boosts motivation and cultivates critical thinking skills.

Beyond nurturing authentic skills, poetry assessments also offer a built-in safeguard against plagiarism and cheating. The creative and personal nature of poetry makes it extremely difficult for students to plagiarise or outsource their work. Composing an original poem requires learners to actively synthesise concepts and articulate connections in their own words. While traditional essays can be readily copied from sources, it is much harder to do this with an authentic work of poetry without detection. Similarly, the distinctive self-expression and idiosyncratic word choices found in poems are challenging for artificial intelligence to effectively mimic (Rudolph et al, 2023).

At a time of growing concerns over academic dishonesty and contract cheating, poetry assessments present a novel way to stimulate original work that clearly emerges from students' own critical thinking. Furthermore, poetry assessments present exciting opportunities for collaboration and peer learning, with students constructing shared understandings of the subject matter (Iida, 2008).

Poetry also engenders creativity, emotional expression, and the integration of multiple perspectives – capabilities that are invaluable yet often marginalised in conventional assessments

(Hanauer, 2012). This chapter will demonstrate that poetry assessments, when thoughtfully designed and implemented, can help to nurture these essential skills.

While highlighting these advantages, we will also tackle the real and perceived challenges of using poetry for assessment. In doing so, we will demonstrate how with proper planning, clear communication, and the investment of time into this innovative technique, most barriers can be overcome. Our goal is to provide both the inspiration and the practical guidance needed to actualise the potential of poetic assessment across diverse higher educational contexts.

Poetry as authentic assessment

A key advantage of poetry as an assessment tool is its ability to serve as a form of authentic assessment. Unlike traditional tests, authentic assessments require students to demonstrate meaningful application of knowledge, mirroring contexts from outside of academia (Ashford-Rowe et al, 2014).

Rather than standardised tests assessing the recall of isolated facts and concepts, authentic assessments engage students in cognitively demanding tasks, problem-solving, collaboration, and communication. Learners must actively construct knowledge and demonstrate deep understanding, not just the reproduction of information.

In a higher education setting, authentic assessments (not involving poetry) may involve:

- Engineering students designing and prototyping solutions to pressing needs in their local community. This demonstrates applying technical skills to address challenges creatively (Johnston et al, 2007).
- Education students creating lesson plans, microteaching sessions, and reflective analyses of instructional strategies. This provides experience with the genuine work of educators (Maryani et al, 2017).

- Nursing students engaging with case studies that mirror the ambiguity and complexity of clinical contexts. This develops clinical reasoning and judgement (Kossman, 2005).
- Business students developing and pitching an innovative business proposal to their peers. This supports the development of an authentic product tailored to a specific audience (Faherty, 2015).
- Art and design students curating a series of exhibitions in collaboration with studios, venues, and businesses. This gives students a unique sense of independence and professionalism as they work collaboratively with each other (McFadyen and McCullagh, 2015).

These examples illustrate the breadth of possibilities for authentic assessment within higher education. The unifying thread is facilitating opportunities for students to create, design, evaluate, argue, perform, or produce shareable products that encourage meaningful learning, rather than just memorisation and test-taking abilities. Poetry assessments can help to integrate these higher-order skills, providing opportunities for students to connect academic concepts to their personal experiences and interests.

For instance, a poetry assessment in a sociology course might involve students selecting a salient concept like inequality, socialisation, or poverty, then authoring a poem exploring how it manifests in their own communities. This exercise would necessitate grappling with abstract theory, relating it to lived realities, then articulating analytical insights creatively. The poetic form adds an additional layer of challenge, requiring careful word choice and integration of imagery to convey complex ideas succinctly.

Similarly, in an undergraduate developmental psychology course, students could maintain a poetry journal documenting their observations and reflections on child development concepts based on their encounters. For such an assessment, students could be asked to compose poems reflecting on observations of children displaying behaviours aligned with theories discussed in class, such as Piaget's stages of cognitive development (Ojose, 2008) or Erikson's stages of psychosocial development (Maree, 2022). The poems would need to connect concrete observations of children in their families, neighbourhoods, or placements to abstract psychological theories. For example, a haiku could describe a moment illustrating a child in the preoperational stage of development, followed by a reflection tying this observation to Piagetian concepts of egocentrism, animism, or symbolic representation (Kesselring and Müller, 2011). Likewise, a free verse poem might be used to depict a child's expressions of autonomy, linking this to Erikson's framework (Maree, 2022). Sharing select journal entries with peers could also enable learning through the comparison of experiences.

Importantly, poetry assessments can be designed to align with desired course outcomes, systematically nurturing the skills and capabilities students require. Their inherent flexibility makes poetry a versatile authentic assessment technique across diverse disciplines. Whether assessing rhetorical skills, research capabilities, critical thinking, or communication acumen, poetry has great potential for eliciting displays of genuine comprehension.

Despite general positivity towards authentic assessments, there remain valid criticisms of how such assessments are defined and implemented within a university setting (see, for example, McArthur, 2023). These criticisms argue that much literature conflates authentic assessment with preparation for the workplace, and that doing so risks reducing education solely to economic ends and graduate employability. Additionally, authentic assessments often focus merely on real-world tasks rather than the larger social significance or value of those tasks (not to mention seeming to forget that higher education is itself part of the 'real world'). As such the emphasis remains on individual skill demonstration and self-worth, rather than a students' relationship to society. There is also a danger that such assessments can result in further strengthening societal and workplace injustices rather than challenging them.

Poetry as authentic assessment can address some of these issues by connecting academic concepts to lived experiences, fostering reflection on social values, and giving voice to excluded perspectives. For example, group poetry writing promotes collaboration and shared meaning-making. Thoughtfully designed poetic assessments can elicit demonstrations of learning that engage students as members of society shaping a just future, not just economic actors. As such poetry is a powerful ally in helping to reshape authentic assessment to focus on students' contributions to social wellbeing, not just workplace skills.

Designing poetry assessments

In designing poetry-based assessments, the fundamentals of effective assessment design must not be overlooked.

Constructive alignment is a pivotal concept in assessment design, referring to the intentional mapping of learning outcomes, teaching and learning activities, and assessment tasks (Biggs, 1996). Rather than viewing these elements in isolation, the curriculum is vertically integrated so that each component scaffolds the learning journey towards the defined outcomes.

In the context of poetry assessments, this means starting with the learning outcomes and intentionally designing poetry activities that provide opportunities for students to demonstrate attainment of those outcomes. For instance, a learning outcome related to analysing literary devices might be aligned to a presentation analysing the use of metaphor and imagery in a poem.

Principles of universal design for learning (UDL) should also shape assessment planning, ensuring accessibility for diverse learners. UDL recommends multiple means of representation, engagement, and expression (Rose et al, 2006). This translates to offering learner choice in assessment formats, providing flexibility in timing and settings, and scaffolding tasks to activate prior knowledge.

Specifically for poetry assessments, UDL principles can make these evaluations more inclusive and accessible. This can be achieved by using collaborative platforms, sharing exemplars to provide clear models, and encouraging creative multimedia responses. By incorporating poetry into assessments, educators can address different learning preferences and needs, making the assessments more engaging and accessible. This approach ensures that poetry assessments are not just a means to evaluate learning, but also a tool to support and include all learners, regardless of their backgrounds or abilities.

As discussed in the previous section, assessments with authentic societal relevance go beyond workplace skills to consider students' roles as social members. As McArthur (2023) argues, authenticity involves nurturing a student's potential to contribute to social justice, civic renewal, and community wellbeing. Poetic assessments can prompt learners to connect academic concepts to lived experiences and social issues. For instance, students could be asked to use primary sources to create a blackout poem (see Chapter 2) on the topic of climate justice, with the ensuing societal perspective helping to reorient any assessment beyond narrow economic ends.

Several key decisions shape effective poetry assessments. Firstly, how will poetry be incorporated – through reading and analysing existing poems, writing original works, critiquing peers' writing, or a blend of approaches? For instance, asking students to author poems makes for an engaging creative challenge, while critiquing previously published poems develops analytical skills. As already discussed, the approach chosen should closely align to any learning outcomes and consider the needs of your learners.

In a literature module, students could be tasked with writing an original poem that demonstrates their analysis of key themes and literary devices in a prose work they have studied. For instance, to demonstrate their understanding of metaphor usage in a novel, learners might craft a poem rich in metaphors that mirror those used by the author. This creative writing challenge requires learners to first comprehend and then imitate the literary techniques under study.

In a healthcare module, students might engage in the peer critiquing of poems reflecting on the emotional impact of clinical experiences. By sharing and giving feedback on each other's poetic expressions, learners can develop nuanced communication skills and perspective-taking. Guidance on delivering constructive criticism is crucial for this collaborative task (see the next section).

By means of an example, imagine a module entitled 'Prehistoric art: origins and transitions' as part of an MA in Early prehistory and human origins. As one of the assessments for this module, learners could be tasked with penning a poem that sheds light on the ways in which prehistoric individuals created art. Such a poem should encapsulate their understanding of the intricate interactions between early humans and their tools, by morphing information into compelling narration. This creative endeavour encourages students to synthesise their knowledge into a form that is more engaging and memorable than mere memorisation. The poem could follow any structural format – a haiku, limerick, free verse – providing it accurately and creatively enlightens readers on the use of instruments in prehistoric times. As an example of what such a poem might look like, here is one in free verse that was written by Sam, inspired by research which has found evidence of the first prehistoric wind instruments (Davin et al, 2023).

Symphony of the Stone Age

Ancient souls we recollect,
crude tools in hand
roughened faces
primitive lives.
Yet beneath our projections

ghosts of music
dance like fleeting dreams,
an echo of melodies
carved from
hollowed bone
to lie in stillness
beneath
the stifling dirt.
Exhumations reset the tone –
a broken window
to melodic
misheard pasts
where roughened faces
tame the air,
flattering birds
luring game
and
trading worlds.
Distant voices
in the wind
revel once more
in song.

Across disciplines, careful decisions around reading, writing, critiquing, or analysing poetry enable diverse opportunities to demonstrate learning while nurturing creativity and communication.

Robust support structures are vital for enabling student success with poetry-based assessments. Providing marking rubric expectations early, and co-creating rubrics with students' input, enhances clarity, while detailed rubrics also promote reliable grading across students, modules, and markers.

When co-creating marking rubrics, establishing an inclusive and trusting environment is critical for successful collaboration between learners and educators (Smith et al, 2021). Start by providing context about any learning outcomes and academic standards to ground the discussion. Then bring students and teachers together to jointly generate rubric criteria, encouraging students to share diverse assessment experiences that inform the process. Emphasise rubrics as learning tools, not just assessment mechanisms, and allow sufficient time for rich discussion as the group works to find consensus on clear language and calibrated expectations. Frame rubric development as an iterative process open to future revisions rather than a one-time activity, keeping the focus on enhancing transparency, understanding, and assessment literacy, not on perfecting artistic expression. Throughout the process, actively listen to all voices and value the knowledge that both learners and educators contribute when given the opportunity to work as partners.

When assessing poetry assignments, it is important for educators not to solely judge the artistic or aesthetic quality of any original poems. Rather, the focus should be on assessing the students' ability to engage with the material and convey meaning and understanding through their poetic expressions. For example, reassure your students that you are not judging their creative writing skills, but instead looking for evidence of critical thinking and knowledge application related to the key concepts that are being assessed. Doing so will help nurture participation from students who may be hesitant to share more interpretive forms of expression. The goal is not award-winning poetry, but rather meaningful engagement and learning through the process of conveying ideas creatively (see Chapter 2, for a further discussion of good enough poetry).

Formative assessment is particularly important for scaffolding success with poetry-based tasks. Unlike summative assessment which evaluates learning at the end, formative assessment provides ongoing feedback to guide improvement during the learning process (William, 2011). For poetry assignments, this includes activities like reflective journals, draft workshops, and peer reviews.

Deliberately embedding recurring formative assessment activities throughout an assessment cycle sustains student motivation, monitors incremental growth, and tailors support. Rather than a high-stakes final assignment, students thereby receive regular feedback to scaffold their success (see the next section). Formative assessment also gives educators insights into learner challenges to address through instruction. In other words, poetry assessments accompanied by robust formative practices create an empowering and enlightening learning experience.

As discussed in Chapter 2, appropriate scaffolding eases entry for students hesitant about engaging with poetry. Preliminary activities like annotating poems, discussing interpretations, and analysing exemplars build confidence. Sentence starters, fill-in-the-blank templates, and example poems provide supportive structures for writing. Likewise, flexible deadlines, low-stakes practice, and opportunities for revision act to accommodate diverse abilities. Providing this scaffolding enables all students to shine when demonstrating their learning through poetry, no matter what their previous encounters with the medium might have been.

Student involvement also enriches poetry assessments. Rather than a top-down process, learners can be involved in co-constructing assignments tailored to their diverse backgrounds and interests. For instance, eliciting student-suggested prompts that link learning outcomes to their own cultures and lived experiences results in poetry tasks that feel personally relevant. Similarly, co-creating marking rubrics collaboratively establishes shared understandings of success criteria and gives students ownership and agency over the evaluation process, while peer reviews of drafts enable rich reciprocal feedback, developing analytical and communication abilities on both sides of the exchange.

Building on this, managing such intricate scaffolding in large modules and courses with hundreds to thousands of students poses significant challenges. The scalability of involving students in co-construction and peer reviews becomes complex with larger cohorts. To address this, educators could segment larger classes into smaller tutorial or workshop groups, to enable more manageable peer interactions. Ensuring students' buy-in for such interactions is crucial; this can be achieved by clearly linking participation to grade incentives or other recognitions. Additionally, a dedicated module or workshop series focusing on developing peer-review skills might be necessary to equip learners (especially undergraduate students) with the requisite skills, as many may not naturally possess them upon entering university.

Imagine that you are the module leader for a first-year undergraduate module entitled 'The science of midwifery', which is part of a 3-year Bachelor of Midwifery course. Your learning outcomes might be as follows:

1. By the end of the module, students will demonstrate a comprehensive understanding of the scientific principles and practices underpinning midwifery, including anatomy, physiology, and the stages of childbirth.
2. Students will be able to critically evaluate and apply evidence-based practices in midwifery, discerning between traditional practices and those grounded in scientific research.
3. Students will illustrate the ability to integrate knowledge from related scientific disciplines, such as biology, genetics, and nutrition, to provide holistic care to both the mother and the newborn.
4. Drawing from both scientific knowledge and personal experiences, students will demonstrate reflective thinking skills to explore and articulate their understanding and emotional response to complex midwifery scenarios.

You might then decide to use poetry to assess Learning Outcome 4 (LO4), for example by asking the students to do the following task:

> Compose a poem that captures a midwifery scenario where both scientific knowledge and personal emotions intersect. Your poem should reflect an understanding of the physiological processes involved while also conveying the emotional complexities that midwives often navigate. This exercise aims to assess your ability to merge scientific insights with reflective thought in a creative format.

A sample rubric for this assignment is presented in Table 3.1, which delineates the criteria for assessment, ensuring that both the scientific understanding and reflective depth of the students' submissions are evaluated. This rubric is structured to guide educators in discerning the depth of students' comprehension and their ability to articulate complex scenarios through poetic expression. Note that these criteria are strongly linked to synthesis and reflection, rather than aesthetics or creative talent.

When introducing this unique assessment to the students, you would need to underscore its objectives clearly, emphasising that the focus is not on their poetic prowess but on their ability to synthesise scientific understanding with introspective thought in a reflective manner.

Given the novelty of this assignment for many students, it would also be necessary to scaffold their learning experience. This could be done with preliminary workshops to acquaint students with the rudiments of poetry and its potential intersection with midwifery. To foster a supportive environment, peer review sessions could also be encouraged. This collaborative approach would allow students to share drafts, gather diverse perspectives, and refine their submissions based on constructive feedback.

If framed correctly, this poetry assignment could be a transformative experience, provided it was introduced with clarity and accompanied by a robust support structure.

Table 3.1: Rubric for poetry assessment on 'the science of midwifery', with scores reflective of the UK higher education classification system

Criteria	First class (70–100%)	2:1 (60–69%)	2:2 (50–59%)	Third class (40–49%)	Fail (0–39%)
Scientific accuracy	Demonstrates an outstanding understanding of the physiological processes in the described scenario.	Displays a solid grasp of the physiological processes with minor inaccuracies.	Shows a satisfactory understanding with some significant errors or omissions.	Demonstrates limited understanding.	Major inaccuracies or misunderstandings.
Reflection and personal insight	Provides profound personal insights, displaying a deep emotional connection to the scenario.	Offers meaningful personal reflections with good depth.	Presents some reflection but could be more insightful.	Offers limited personal reflection.	Minimal to no reflection or insight.
Integration of scientific knowledge	Seamlessly integrates scientific knowledge with reflective thought in an exceptional manner.	Integrates scientific knowledge and reflection well, with slight disconnects.	Some attempt at integrating science and reflection but feels somewhat disjointed.	Struggles to integrate knowledge and reflection.	Lack of coherent integration.
Clarity and coherence	The poem is clear, coherent, and effectively conveys the intended message without ambiguity.	The poem is mostly clear and coherent with minor ambiguities.	The poem has moments of clarity but is occasionally unclear or fragmented.	The poem is often unclear or disjointed.	The poem is consistently unclear or off-topic.
Relevance to midwifery scenario	The described scenario is directly relevant to midwifery and displays an outstanding understanding of the field.	The scenario is relevant with good detail but could be more specific.	The scenario is somewhat relevant but lacks specific details or depth.	The scenario is vaguely related to midwifery.	Scenario is unrelated or lacks relevance.

EXERCISE 3.1: DESIGN YOUR OWN POETRY ASSESSMENT

Estimated engagement time: Variable, may take several hours spread over days (we recommend allocating at least 4–6 hours).

Aim: To design a meaningful poetry assessment that aligns with a module's learning outcomes and supports students in demonstrating their understanding and skills.

Objectives:

- Identify pivotal learning outcomes for assessment.
- Choose an appropriate poetry engagement approach.
- Draft a clear task description and create a rubric.
- Plan supportive structures and incorporate student input.

Output: A well-structured poetry assessment task with clear instructions, a rubric, and planned support structures.

Type of exercise: Individual, with potential group collaboration in Step 6.

Materials needed:

- Module documentation.
- Writing materials (pen and paper or digital device).
- Access to example poems and other relevant resources.

Activity:

Step 1: Determine learning outcomes

Carefully consult the module documentation and identify two or three pivotal learning outcomes you want to assess through this poetry assignment. Outcomes should reflect the core knowledge and higher-order skills you aim to develop in students through the module. The outcomes serve as the foundation for assessment design, so reflect on which of them need the most evidence of student proficiency.

Step 2: Choose an approach

Consider how students will engage with poetry. Will they analyse existing poems, write original works, critique peer writing, or be tasked with a blend of approaches? Match the approach directly to the skills and capabilities outlined in the learning outcomes. For instance, an analytic task might be used to evaluate critical thinking, while original poetry could be used to evidence creativity or synthesis. Blending approaches, like analysing then emulating a poem's style, allows multidimensional demonstration of skills.

Step 3: Draft the task description

Compose a prompt that provides clear instructions, so students understand the task, but which allows flexibility for creative responses. Link the prompt explicitly to the specified learning outcome(s) so the task guides students to demonstrate the relevant knowledge and proficiencies. Share the prompts early so learners have time to generate ideas and ask clarifying questions.

Step 4: Create a rubric

Develop a rubric with four or five criteria tied directly to the learning outcomes being evaluated. Include poetry-specific criteria and others corresponding to the assignment approach, assigning point values for each criterion reflective of its relative importance. Provide the rubric upfront so students can align their work to your expectations. You might use Table 3.1 to help you in your development.

Step 5: Plan support structures

Consider scaffolds that will build confidence in students hesitant about poetry. Useful strategies include modelling poetic analysis, sharing exemplars of original poetry with your commentary, and facilitating collaborative peer workshopping of poem drafts. Create an environment where students feel supported to succeed rather than doomed to fail.

Step 6: Incorporate student input

Increase engagement by inviting students to co-develop your rubric and suggest relevant prompt ideas. However, be sure to manage the scope of their input so that academic standards and expectations are maintained.

Step 7: Align to principles of inclusive assessment

Verify that the assessment workload and timing is reasonable, instructions are clear, formats are accessible to diverse learners, and accommodations are made for students needing flexibility. Apply principles of UDL to ensure all students can meaningfully engage with the assessment.

Step 8: Confirm authentic relevance

Reflect on how this poetry assessment nurtures skills and knowledge valuable beyond the classroom. Adjust the task design if needed to strengthen authentic application and relevance to transformative societal aims.

Poetry and feedback

High-quality feedback is not an isolated event but an ongoing dialogue supporting student development (Carless et al, 2011). Optimal feedback is proactive and personalised, providing actionable insights students can use (Winstone et al, 2017). To enhance effectiveness, feedback should delineate subsequent actions rather than merely assess present performance. Ideally, it should strike a balance between acknowledging strengths and addressing areas for development, as this facilitates a more constructive learning experience (Lizzio and Wilson, 2008).

The feedback delivery method also influences its potential effectiveness. For example, oral feedback allows nuanced explanations and interpersonal connection (Ice et al, 2010). Likewise, as will be discussed, peer feedback can significantly widen evaluative perspectives, providing that learners have sufficient support and scaffolding (Nicol et al, 2014; Huisman et al, 2019; Simonsmeier et al, 2020).

Ultimately, students must have opportunities to process, clarify, and apply feedback (Carless and Boud, 2018), which is why sustaining feedback conversations throughout the lifecycle of an assessment (from when it is first introduced to when it is marked) fuels intrinsic motivation and self-efficacy among learners (Winstone and Carless, 2020).

Overall, the foundations of effective feedback find a natural fit with poetry's personal nature. Specificity, constructive tone, learner-centred insight, and ongoing dialogue will empower learners to refine their poetic voice and harness creative expression. Poetry's subjectivity and evocative nature call for feedback attuned to the nuances of each student's expression. For example, when feeding back on assessments asking students to write poetry, responses should focus on the ways in which the student has tried to explore the topic and/or their lived experience, rather than strictly be focused on the aesthetic 'merit' of the piece. Providing generic commentary disconnected from any intimate details (or the marking rubric) risks ringing especially hollow.

While affirming creative strengths to encourage risk-taking, feedback must also challenge areas needing development in a constructive manner. Delivering responses verbally through either one-on-one dialogues or audio recordings allows nuanced explanations about poetic choices that can sometimes get lost in written feedback alone. In some instances, a multimodal approach combining written summary documents with personal exchanges can further enrich the depth of the feedback as well as the learning experience for both the student and educator.

Peer feedback adds invaluable learner perspectives to complement educator insights into poetic assessments. However, just as they might need help developing their poetic literacies, students may also need support providing constructive and effective feedback to their peers (Van der Pol et al, 2008).

Initially, you (as an educator) should explicitly highlight and model what constitutes effective feedback. Alongside this, co-develop standards for delivering feedback that are both respectful and specific, rooted in the rubric criteria. It is essential to demonstrate to students what effective feedback looks like, especially in the early stages of this process. Similarly, facilitating reflection after students receive feedback can help them better understand effective and inclusive practice. Recognising the process students undertake when writing poems, not just the poem that is created, provides insight into their poetic and educational development. With the appropriate scaffolding, students can provide feedback on each other's draft work and final submissions. This process not only empowers their learning experience but also prepares them to help each other grow as poets and learners.

EXERCISE 3.2: DESIGNING EFFECTIVE FEEDBACK

Estimated engagement time: Variable, may take several hours spread over days (we recommend allocating at least 3–4 hours).

Aim: To create a structured feedback system for the poetry assessment designed in Exercise 3.1, aligning feedback with learning outcomes to support student growth, and understanding.

Objectives:

- Draft criteria for high-quality feedback aligned to learning outcomes.
- Provide examples of effective feedback.
- Develop activities to facilitate constructive peer feedback exchanges.

Output: A structured feedback system including criteria for effective feedback, examples of feedback, peer feedback activities, and a schedule for feedback reflection and response.

Type of exercise: Individual, with potential group collaboration in Steps 4 and 6.

Materials needed:

- Rubric and learning outcomes from Exercise 3.1.
- Writing materials (pen and paper or digital device).
- Exemplar submissions for providing sample feedback.

Activity:

Step 1: Revisit the rubric and learning outcomes

Review the rubric and learning outcomes that guided your assessment design in Exercise 3.1. What were the core knowledge and skills you sought to evaluate through this poetry assessment?

Step 2: Draft criteria for effective feedback aligned to learning outcomes

Outline what high-quality feedback would look like for this assessment by aligning criteria to learning outcomes. When providing feedback on poetry assessments, the criteria should be aligned to the intended learning outcomes rather than just evaluating the poem itself. For example, if assessing the use of metaphorical language, high-quality feedback would point out where metaphors effectively enrich meaning and demonstrate critical thinking. It would suggest how ineffective metaphors could be rewritten to convey the intended ideas and knowledge more clearly. Going beyond just identifying strong and weak metaphors in the poem, effective feedback should evaluate how well the metaphors highlight the student's ability to express complex concepts creatively. The goal is to provide feedback that assesses and supports the development of critical thinking skills and poetic literacy, rather than just the perceived quality of the poem.

Step 3: Provide samples of quality feedback on exemplars

Create examples of feedback that meet (and miss) your criteria on sample submissions. Annotate exemplars to illustrate how to give constructive, specific commentary targeting improvement, and share these with students at the start of the assessment cycle.

Step 4: Develop activities to support peer feedback exchanges

Design scaffolded activities to prepare students for giving constructive peer feedback. Useful strategies include co-developing standards, modelling feedback, and sharing exemplars. Peer feedback works best when framed as mutually beneficial skills development for all.

Step 5: Allow students time to assimilate and respond to feedback through reflection

Build in class time for students to read feedback, note takeaways, formulate potential revisions, and ask clarifying questions. Encourage them to think about what this feedback might mean for future assessments.

Step 6: Offer multiple modes – oral, written, peer – for comprehensive feedback

Strive to provide layered feedback through a blend of individual oral conversations, peer workshops, detailed written comments, and student self-review.

Poetry can also be harnessed to deliver dynamic feedback on more conventional assignments. Rather than only prose-based comments, students could receive responses in the form of poems, highlighting their work's strengths and areas for refinement. This artistic approach encourages us as educators to distil our commentary into concise yet evocative language.

For instance, you might summarise a lab report's key insights in a rhyming stanza, praising the clarity of explanations through metaphor, and suggesting improvements through vivid imagery. Students could then reply with a poem mapping how they plan to implement the feedback. This exchange enlivens meaning making and builds engagement. Poetry feedback adds creativity, demands pointed precision, and enables learners to parse feedback by translating it into their own poetic responses. Similarly, the constraints of specific metres can provide helpful boundaries when synthesising assessments for formative purposes.

While the poetic feedback approach might initially sound demanding, it does not necessitate lengthy compositions or exhaustive corrections. Instead, the focus is on concise, impactful exchanges. Implementing this method could be reserved for key assignments or milestones rather than every assessment. Furthermore, educators might opt to use this approach in smaller tutorial groups or workshops rather than in larger lecture settings. The aim is not to add to the workload but to make the feedback process more memorable and engaging for all.

Purposefully incorporating poetry into feedback workflows, even on non-poetic assessments, infuses feedback with more humanity, imagination, and dialogue. Students gain confidence in processing feedback and formulating plans for growth, and in doing so poetry becomes both a medium for effective feedback and an empowering lens for other learners to interpret and act upon.

Challenges and barriers

While poetry presents exciting opportunities to reimagine assessment, implementing such an innovative approach also surfaces obstacles that educators should acknowledge and proactively address.

One potential barrier is a lack of confidence among both students and teachers in composing high-quality poetry, as those unaccustomed to creative writing may doubt their skills. However, providing strong scaffolding through strategies like sharing exemplar poems co-created with previous cohorts, outlining expectations clearly in marking rubrics, facilitating constructive peer support in draft workshopping, and offering initial structures through sentence starters, fill-in-the-blank templates, and model poems can help lessen any concerns about poetic prowess. As discussed throughout this book, the goal is not poetic perfection but learner engagement, so focusing the assessment on knowledge application and meaning making over writing technique, coupled with reassurances that the focus rests on conveying understanding through verse as opposed to judging artistic ability, can help nurture willingness to experiment with poetry among those who are initially hesitant.

Assessors also require training and calibration to evaluate student poetry consistently and limit subjective bias, which activities like co-marking submissions across graders and engaging in moderation discussions can promote. Assessors may also need to be encouraged to overcome preconceptions that poetry cannot rigorously demonstrate academic knowledge. Carefully designed rubrics outlining expectations tied back to learning outcomes prove instrumental in building confidence in poetry's academic value, with guidance for assessors and moderators to focus extensive commentary on how well students have synthesised knowledge creatively against learning outcomes, rather than only judging artistic merit.

There might also be concerns about poetry assessments lacking rigour and transparency. However, well-constructed rubrics integrated with learning outcomes can help to reinforce academic standards. Poetry tasks frequently evaluate higher order thinking like connecting ideas, reflecting critically, and applying concepts imaginatively, so creativity and risk-taking should be celebrated not penalised in marking, while gathering ongoing feedback and providing exemplars helps alleviate misperceptions.

A further critique is that poetry grants inherent advantages to more talented writers, yet providing appropriate scaffolding and yielding flexibility for multimedia responses can help to cultivate poetic skills in all students. In doing so, we need to disconnect writing technique from knowledge application in rubric design and marking, alongside promoting a growth mindset that poem writing is a teachable skill rather than a fixed aptitude.

These barriers accentuate the need for training, for communities of practice to share effective practices, and for the incremental implementation of such assessments with continual feedback and evaluation. With informed planning, the concerns around poetry-based assessment can be mitigated to unlock its immense learning benefits.

Further study

The Further study section in this chapter has been designed to provide a deeper understanding of using poetry for your own assessment and feedback practices.

Conduct a needs analysis for authentic assessment. First, identify authentic needs by observing student challenges, consulting industry on workforce gaps, and researching civic issues. Target two or three priority needs that either fit with or challenge the learning outcomes for your module, speaking to affected communities to understand their perspectives. Next, work with one of these communities (including students) to develop a poetry prompt addressing the prioritised need through applied knowledge; for example, a civic poetry project raising awareness of the challenges faced by a marginalised group. Ensure the prompt stretches students to apply learning socially, and not just exhibit comprehension of any learning outcomes.

Co-create feedback criteria. Collaborate with your learners to establish standards of excellence for giving feedback on a particular poetry assessment. Develop an agreed-upon checklist of desired criteria together and discuss the most effective and appropriate mode(s) of delivery.

Run an assessment workshop. First, form small groups of four or five students. Provide each group with copies of a sample poetry assignment submitted by students from a previous cohort, along with the assessment rubric. If samples are not available, have groups generate their own mock submissions or create your own in advance. Give the groups about 20 minutes to review the assignments through the lens of the rubric, proposing overall grades and justifying these based on the marking criteria. Ask them to draft some feedback, potentially guided by a co-created feedback criterion (discussed earlier). After this analysis period, have groups swap submissions and recommend grades and feedback. Then, reconvene as a class and compare the recommendations. Did groups all evaluate the assignments consistently? Where did interpretations differ and why?

Summary

This chapter has illustrated how poetry can address common assessment pitfalls like disengagement and lack of authenticity. The constraints of the poetic form compel students to craft precise expressions of their learning, demonstrating the depth of their knowledge. Poetry assessments also foster integration of personal contexts, diverse perspectives, and creativity. However, as with any innovative technique, there are barriers to recognise and proactively mitigate. Overall, poetry holds meaningful yet untapped potential to reimagine assessment as the type of enriching, inspiring, and authentic learning experience that can transform a learner's relationship with education. It is hoped the strategies and exemplars provided throughout this chapter will empower you to help bring this vision to life, unlocking some of the possibilities of poetry for authentic, engaging, and inclusive assessment.

As we transition into Chapter 4, we will extend the pedagogical lens applied thus far to explore how poetry might be used in a research context within higher education. In doing so we will highlight the versatility of poetry beyond the classroom, investigating its potential to enrich academic inquiry and discourse, thereby maintaining a coherent thread of exploration from pedagogy to research while keeping aligned with the book's overarching theme of effectively integrating poetry in higher education.

FOUR

Poetry for research in higher education

Chapter highlights

- The potential of poetry in academic research and scholarship.
- Methods and techniques for integrating poetry in research projects.
- Addressing challenges and finding solutions in poetic research.
- Case studies demonstrating the application of poetry in various research contexts.

Introduction

Building on the pedagogical insights of preceding chapters, this chapter aims to illustrate how poetry can contribute creativity to the research process, enhancing engagement and reflection on the human experiences under study. Moreover, we will address potential challenges of such methods, providing pragmatic solutions and bridging discussions from pedagogical applications to research explorations. Through this approach, we aim to extend the discourse from the classroom to the realm of academic inquiry, further evidencing the role that poetry can play in higher education.

The past few decades have seen a profound shift in the research landscape of higher education (Trowler, 2019). Traditionally, the realm of academic research has been one framed around objectivity, rigid methodologies, and scepticism for the subjective (Parker and Jary, 1995). However, we now find ourselves on the brink of a significant renaissance, where the strict contours of research are being gently blurred to accommodate more innovative and nuanced forms of inquiry (Millar, 2016).

As we embark on this investigation of poetry's role in research, let us clarify the scope of our exploration. Our reference to research in this chapter pertains to the realm of higher education as both a discipline and a subject of investigation. Higher education, in its multifaceted existence, presents a rich terrain of inquiry. Whether one is examining pedagogical strategies, analysing curriculum structures, studying student engagement, or investigating administrative processes, higher education offers a broad spectrum of research avenues.

For instance, as educators we may adopt a poetic approach to explore the transition of postgraduate university students, bringing to life their anxieties, victories, and transformations in verse (Aird, 2017). Alternatively, we might choose to construct a poetic narrative from an ethnographic study on the experiences of international students (Zhang, 2021). Similarly, poetry could be employed to capture the dynamics of a unique pedagogical strategy, giving voice to both the educator's vision and the students' reception of it (Iida, 2008). Through these varied examples, it becomes clear how poetry, with its capacity for emotionality and depth, can illuminate the layered complexities inherent in the landscape of higher education.

The potential to inject creativity into the process of academic inquiry offers an invigorating alternative to the sometimes-monotonous rhythms of research. Poetry allows us to express findings with great nuance, to encapsulate the complexities and subtleties of our study subjects that might otherwise remain unarticulated (Roberts et al, 2014). Moreover, the use of poetry in research can serve to make academic findings more accessible and engaging, both within the academic community and to other audiences as well (Illingworth, 2020).

Throughout this chapter we will provide a guided tour of the varied ways that poetry can enhance higher education research. By presenting a series of engaging case studies, we will illustrate how researchers have innovatively employed poetry within their academic pursuits, allowing you to witness the transformative power of poetry in action. These instances will serve not just as inspiration, but also as tangible examples of how poetry can be woven into the fabric of scholarly inquiry.

Moreover, to equip you with the tools necessary to harness the potential of poetry in your own research, we will explore a range of methodologies and techniques specifically tailored for this purpose. These practical guides will aid you in transforming your own academic findings into compelling poetic narratives.

Finally, acknowledging that the incorporation of poetry in research may come with its unique set of challenges, we also provide practical advice and strategies to identify and navigate potential hurdles.

The potential of poetry in higher education research

As we commence our in-depth examination of poetry's potential within higher education research, we turn our gaze towards real studies that have successfully harnessed this medium. By exploring these examples, we aspire to reveal the diverse avenues through which poetry can be used to conduct innovative, effective, and rigorous research.

Case study 4.1: Poetry in action

Key takeaway: Demonstrates poetry's potential as a reflective tool in higher education, fostering a personal understanding of learning experiences in sports coaching students.

The first case study we would like to present is research by Scott John Threlfall (2013), which explores the untapped potential of poetry as a reflective apparatus in the realm of higher education. In this study, Threlfall ventured into an experiment with a group of UK-based students enrolled on a Foundation Degree in Sports Coaching, challenging them to capture their learning experiences in poetic form. The resultant anthology of poems, serving as the data for this research, unveiled both the strengths and limitations of poetry as a tool for reflection.

The students' poems were then categorised into thematic clusters reflecting their learning experiences, encompassing subjects such as meeting deadlines, improving organisational skills, and contending with motivational challenges.

Threlfall's research showed that poetry amplified the students' reflective capability as the act of writing poems coerced them into a mindful consideration of word order. Conversely, the attention paid to crafting the poetic structure slightly distracted from the reflective process, serving as a limitation.

This study gives particular emphasis to the role of feedback in the reflective process. Threlfall posits that while reflection is a staple in academia, a structured process of progressive evaluation and feedback is often missing from the educator's toolkit. This study suggests that future research incorporating poetry for reflection could benefit from titled prompts to shepherd the participants towards more deliberate reflective accounts. Moreover, a longer period dedicated to familiarising participants with the art of poetry (in other words, better scaffolding) could further bolster the reflective process.

Although Threlfall acknowledges the socio-cultural resistance of sports students to poetry, the research indicates that the benefits derived from such practice are manifold. Threlfall concedes that without an effective process, poetry and reflective practice may lead to descriptive accounts. However, depending upon the objective of the activity, this may not necessarily be a drawback. In doing so, he invites sports educators to view creative writing methodologies as an avenue to enhance teaching and learning strategies.

Threlfall's study offers a compelling argument for the incorporation of poetry as a medium for data collection and a catalyst for reflection in higher education. The collection of poems, penned by the students, provides a unique and personal glimpse into their learning experiences, enhancing the research data. The study underscores the potential of poetry as a reflective tool (see Chapter 5), inviting educators and researchers to integrate creative and reflective methods into their teaching and learning strategies.

Case study 4.2: The exotic other

Key takeaway: Examines how poetry and personal narrative can expose and challenge the cultural and academic struggles faced by Muslim female academics in the United States.

The second case study is a poetic autoethnography written by Samah A. Elbelazi and Lama Alharbi (2020). This innovative blend of poetry and personal narrative unfurls a tapestry of cultural experiences, illuminating the intricate trials and tribulations faced by two Muslim female academics working in the United States.

Over the course of a year, the authors produced a collection of emotionally resonant poems which were subsequently organised into three thematic clusters: conceptualising agency, the Muslim ban, and challenging diversity. Each theme forms a chapter of their unfolding narrative, spotlighting their experiences as visibly Muslim women in their classrooms, their fear and uncertainty catalysed by the 2017 executive order banning citizens from certain Muslim-majority countries, and their persistent striving for representation and belonging in the face of perceived exoticism.

These poems serve as poignant portraits of the authors' battles as minorities in public higher education. The Islamic attire, they argue, assumes a potent symbolism of their intersectional identities, particularly within contexts permeated by Islamophobia. Their Muslimness becomes a collective identity that overshadows their individuality, painting a vivid picture of their lived experiences.

Poetry, in this context, transcends the boundaries of research methodology and adopts the role of a therapeutic catalyst. The process of weaving words into verses brings solace to the authors, promoting self-understanding and offering stress relief. Poetry's inherent ability to resonate with human emotions empowers their work, amplifying its influence.

Elbelazi and Alharbi's poetic journey offers invaluable insights into the lived experiences of Muslim women navigating the predominantly Christian/ secular institutions of higher education in the West. Furthermore, this work highlights poetry's role as a medium for introspection and therapeutic relief; it's capacity to articulate and share marginalised narratives makes it a valuable tool specifically in higher education research. The potential here lies in the ability of poetry to evoke and express nuanced perspectives, which can enrich academic inquiries for both educators and learners.

Case study 4.3: Poetry in practice

Key takeaway: Highlights the disciplined use of poetry in academic research, enriching traditional methods with the expressive power of poetry for deeper understanding.

Our final case study is centred on the work conducted by Sam, specifically the written dissertation (Illingworth, 2016) for his MA in Higher Education. We have chosen this case study, because it highlights the potential of poetry not as a research method but as a subject within the academic sphere.

This study centred on the complex issue of student engagement, a widely acknowledged challenge within higher education (Baron and Corbin, 2012). Departing from conventional approaches, Sam introduced a novel angle – fostering a sense of belonging and engagement through the prism of poetry.

To probe this innovative approach, he established 'Poetry in Practice', a two-term poetry collective at Manchester Metropolitan University in the UK (where Sam was at the time employed as a Lecturer). This initiative encouraged a group of students to regularly engage in reading, writing, and sharing poetry, in the process of which they developed a unique sense of community. The effectiveness of this approach was assessed not via poetic methods, but through traditional qualitative research methods: semi-structured interviews and field notes.

From this research, several insights emerged. Interestingly, the students' participation in the poetry sessions was primarily driven by intrinsic motivation, suggesting an authentic affinity for this unorthodox educational experience. Furthermore, these weekly poetry meet-ups were seen as a sanctuary, a comforting respite from the conventional academic grind.

Another pivotal observation was the crucial role of the facilitator, challenging the initial assumption of the facilitator's diminishing involvement as student engagement increased. Instead, the students emphasised the value of the facilitator's ongoing enthusiasm and guidance, in agreement with what Vygotsky (1978) terms the 'more knowledgeable other', in other words, that social learning and development is extended by the support of someone who has a better understanding or higher initial ability level than the learner.

This exploration offers a personalised perspective on the transformative potential of integrating poetry into the fabric of higher education. Here, poetry served more as a subject of research than a research method. The conventional tools of interviews and field notes were employed, while poetry played a pivotal role in fostering an enhanced sense of engagement and community. This case study illustrates how the power of poetry can be harnessed within academic contexts, providing a blueprint for blending traditional research methods with innovative thematic elements.

These three case studies illustrate that poetry can be used with great discipline and methodological soundness. In each of these instances, poetry was not employed as an arbitrary add-on but was carefully interwoven into the research design, serving specific and thoughtful purposes.

Poetry's strength lies in its ability to encapsulate the essence of human experiences in a manner that pure data often cannot. This does not undermine the validity or rigour of the research; on the contrary, it enriches it. It allows us to grapple with the complexities, the nuances, and the profundities of our subjects of study, painting a fuller, more holistic picture. Therefore, the use of poetry in higher education research is not only justifiable but is recommended as a compelling, innovative approach to enhancing the depth and breadth of our scholarly endeavours.

As we venture into the next section of this chapter, our aim is to equip you, the reader, with the practical knowledge and skills to weave the unique attributes of poetry into your own research endeavours in higher education. We shall unpack practical methodologies, illuminate effective practices, and offer guidance to ease the integration of poetry into your own academic research. Proceeding further, we shall engage in an in-depth exploration of the practical dimensions of formulating poetic research methodologies.

Methods and techniques for using poetry in academic research

In conducting any form of research, understanding the relationship between research method and research methodology is essential. A research method refers to the specific tool used, like interviews, observations, or questionnaires, while a methodology outlines the reasoning for selecting that tool. When poetry is used as a research method, it falls squarely into the qualitative research domain, which seeks to understand experiences, interpretations, and the meanings individuals assign to their own realities, highlighting the depth and richness of these experiences. The interpretive nature of poetry aligns beautifully with this approach, offering a fresh lens through which to understand our world and providing nuanced insights that may be overlooked in quantitative data.

Every piece of academic research is anchored in a set of beliefs about knowledge and reality, referred to as epistemology and ontology, respectfully. Understanding these philosophical foundations helps us appreciate how poetry can fit into this intricate web of knowledge. Poetry resonates with a constructivist epistemology, which posits that knowledge is a subjective interpretation, shaped by our personal experiences (Howe and Berv, 2000). From an ontological perspective, poetry aligns with a relativist view, supporting the existence of multiple realities, each one sculpted by individual experiences and perspectives (Gura, 1992).

This link between poetry and research philosophy is not just a theoretical detour; it is a crucial step towards understanding how poetry can be practically applied in research. It outlines how poetry can naturally weave into our research efforts, helping unravel complex research subjects.

Having established the philosophical alignment between poetry and research, it is time to tackle the practical implications. Within the realm of higher education research, how can we effectively integrate poetry and scholarly study? What methods can we employ to ensure the integrity of this amalgamation?

Poetic inquiry involves using poetry as a tool throughout the research process – from data collection to analysis and presentation of findings. Researchers may engage participants in writing poems to capture their experiences, then analyse these poetic data to identify themes. Crafting poems also aids in synthesising and communicating research insights. For example, a researcher might ask first-year undergraduate students to write poems about their experiences of university. The researcher would then analyse these poems to identify themes, such as the challenges of adjusting to university life, the search for identity, and the excitement of new beginnings (Illingworth and Radhakrishnan, 2023). Similarly, we might use poetic inquiry to explore the experiences of people working in higher education. The researcher would invite participants to write poetry about their experiences and the poems would then be analysed to identify themes, such as the pressure to publish, the fear of failure, and the challenges of balancing research, teaching, and service (Illingworth and Grimwood, 2024).

Poetic transcription transforms interview transcripts or field notes into poems or poetic sequences. This is a process where the precise sentences spoken by participants are repurposed, yet instead of merely presenting them as block quotes or paraphrasing, they are creatively reshaped and presented in a poetic format. This distillation into verse illuminates the essence of participants' narratives. The researcher carefully selects excerpts and restructures the words to build an evocative poem while retaining authenticity. For example, a researcher might transcribe an interview with Indigenous academic women about their experiences in higher education (Thunig and Jones, 2021). The researcher would then transform the transcript into a poem, using poetic techniques such as imagery, metaphor, and rhythm to capture the emotional intensity of each learner's story. A researcher might also transcribe field notes from an ethnographic study of international graduate student mothers about their experiences of juggling motherhood and academic demands (Zhang, 2020). In turning these notes into poetry, they would attempt to encapsulate the emotional depth of these mothers' narratives, thereby providing an immersive experience of their unique journey in higher education.

Poetic autoethnography uses personal poetry writing throughout the research process as a means of reflexivity. Writing autobiographical poems enables the researcher to be introspective about their positionality and interpretations. This poetic self-study enriches the research process. For example, a researcher might write a series of poems about their own experiences of adapting to different cultures (Keleş, 2023). These poems would explore the researcher's emotions, thoughts, and memories of these experiences, contextualising this with the current and future challenges faced by higher education. A researcher might alternatively draft a poem about their experiences of conducting research on a sensitive topic, such as expressing experiences and confronting ableism and discrimination on campus (Robinson, 2017). Such a poem might explore the researcher's own emotions and thoughts about this topic, as well as the challenges of conducting such research.

The three methods described are not the only ones that can be used for poetic inquiry in higher education research. Other methods include:

- **Poetic collage**. This method involves creating a poem by combining different elements of text, such as interview transcripts, field notes, and poems written by participants (Sanchez and Brown, 2023).

- **Found poetry as literature review**. This method involves selecting key phrases, sentences, or passages from primary sources (hence 'found' poetry) and rearranging them into a poetic format (Prendergast, 2006).
- **Poetic conversation**. This method entails crafting poems in response to each other's writings to generate an insightful poetic dialogue (Faulkner, 2016).
- **Communal poetry writing**. This collaborative method brings together participants to co-create poems reflecting their shared experiences (Smart and Loads, 2017).

These are just a few examples of the ways that poetry can be used in higher education research, and which are presented in Table 4.1 for ease of reference. Poetry as a research method is a flexible and creative approach that can be used to explore a wide range of topics. It is important to note that these methods are not mutually exclusive. A researcher might use a combination of methods in their research, such as using poetic inquiry to collect and analyse the data, before using poetic transcription to synthesise and present the findings. The choice of method will depend on the specific research question and the context of the research. However, all these methods share a common goal: using poetry to explore the experiences of higher education in a way that is both creative and rigorous.

In integrating poetry into academic research, especially when involving students, it is essential to navigate ethical considerations with care and thoughtfulness. This includes ensuring informed consent, where participants understand the nature of the research and their involvement in it. Ethical approval from relevant committees is always required to uphold the integrity of the research, particularly in studies that explore personal experiences or sensitive topics.

Power dynamics between educators and learners must be carefully managed to maintain a respectful and equitable environment. Researchers should be mindful of their influence and strive to create a space where students feel comfortable and

Table 4.1: Summary of methods for integrating poetry into higher education research

Method	Description
Poetic inquiry	Uses poetry throughout the research process, from data collection to analysis and presentation. Might involve participants or researchers writing poems, and could be followed by thematic or case-based analysis.
Poetic transcription	Involves transforming interview transcripts or field notes into poems or poetic sequences. This method creatively reshapes spoken sentences or field observations into poetic formats, emphasising the emotional essence of participants' narratives.
Poetic autoethnography	Uses personal poetry writing as a means of reflexivity throughout the research process. Autobiographical poems enable researchers to introspect about their positionality and interpretations, enriching the research.
Poetic collage	This method combines various textual elements like interview transcripts, field notes, and participant-written poems into a singular poetic piece.
Found poetry as literature review	Involves selecting key phrases, sentences, or passages from primary sources and rearranging them into a poetic format to conduct a literature review.
Poetic conversation	The crafting of poems in response to each other's writings, fostering a poetic dialogue that generates insights.
Communal poetry writing	A collaborative method where participants co-create poems, reflecting their shared experiences.

safe to express themselves without any pressure or bias. This ethical mindfulness is integral to the use of poetry in higher education research, ensuring that the creative exploration of experiences through poetry is conducted in a responsible and respectful manner.

You should also consider safeguarding measures and provide appropriate support for people who may find the process distressing or uncover personal issues, such as those related to mental health and wellbeing. Be prepared to signpost participants to relevant support services, such as counselling or mental health resources, and create an environment where people feel safe and supported. This support mechanism is vital in research involving emotive and personal content like poetry, ensuring that participants are cared for and their wellbeing is prioritised throughout the research process.

However, it is also important to highlight the potential positive impacts of engaging with poetry in this context. Engaging with poetry can be a therapeutic and empowering experience, offering participants a unique avenue for self-expression and emotional exploration. The act of creating and sharing poetry can foster a sense of community, resilience, and personal growth, contributing positively to mental wellbeing. By acknowledging both the challenges and benefits, we ensure a balanced approach, prioritising participant care while recognising the transformative power of poetry in research.

As discussed earlier, you should also consider the effect that reading and analysing these poems might have on you, the researcher, as engaging deeply with emotive content can evoke personal responses or reflections. The process of engaging with poetry often touches upon sensitive or profound themes, which can resonate on a personal level. It is important to be aware of and prepared for the potential emotional impact this might have on your own mental and emotional state. Practicing self-reflection and self-care, and seeking support when needed, can help to maintain your own wellbeing while conducting this kind of research. Being attuned to your reactions can also enrich your understanding of the research material and contribute to a more empathetic and nuanced approach to your study.

EXERCISE 4.1: A POETIC LITERATURE REVIEW

Estimated engagement time: Variable, may span over a few days (we recommend allocating at least 8–10 hours).

Aim: To transform academic insights into a poetic expression, thereby enabling a creative exploration and understanding of a chosen topic within higher education.

Objectives:

- Select and engage with key academic sources on a chosen topic.
- Extract significant phrases or sentences that encapsulate core ideas or findings.
- Create a poetic summary and synthesis of the literature, exploring the essence of the chosen topic.
- Reflect on the process and the insights gained from this creative approach to literature review.

Output: A poem that encapsulates a literature review on a selected higher education topic, along with a reflective piece on the process and insights gained.

Type of exercise: Individual.

Materials needed:

- Access to academic sources (library, online databases, and so on).
- Writing materials (pen and paper or digital device).

Activity:

Step 1: Choose a higher education topic

To start, select a topic within the field of higher education that interests you and that you would like to learn more about. This could be anything from online learning and student mental health to academic integrity and university governance.

Step 2: Select key sources

Next, identify and select five or six key academic sources about your chosen topic. These can be academic journal articles, books, or reputable reports. Try to choose a mix of sources that offer diverse perspectives and insights on your chosen topic.

Step 3: Read and highlight

Read these sources, and as you read, highlight memorable phrases, statements, or findings. Look for quotes that encapsulate significant ideas, findings, or arguments presented in the literature.

Step 4: Extract key points

After reading and highlighting, go back through each source and extract the phrases or sentences you have highlighted. Write these down in a separate document or sheet of paper.

Step 5: Create your poem

Now comes the creative part. Take all the extracts you have gathered and start arranging them in a way that feels right to you. Do not be afraid to repeat phrases or rearrange words and remember that your poem does not need to rhyme. The goal is to create a summary and synthesis of the literature that not only conveys the key points but also captures the essence of what the literature is saying about your chosen topic. You might find it helpful to group similar themes or ideas together, or you might prefer a more chronological approach.

Step 6: Reflect on your process

After creating your poem, take some time to reflect on how this process of writing a poetic literature review differed from writing a traditional literature review. How did the process of selecting and arranging phrases impact your understanding of the literature? Did the poetry-writing process change how you engage with academic texts? Did the final poem reveal any new insights or connections that you had not noticed when reading the literature in its original form?

EXERCISE 4.2: DESIGN A POETIC RESEARCH PROJECT

Estimated engagement time: Variable, depending on the depth and scope of the research.

Aim: To design and conduct a research project using poetry as a research method to explore a specific topic within higher education.

Objectives:

- Formulate a research question based on observations within the classroom environment.
- Select an appropriate method for conducting the research.
- Design the study, ensuring ethical considerations are met.
- Conduct the study, analyse the data, and write up the findings.

Output: A completed research project that uses poetry to explore a specified topic, with findings documented in a written report.

Type of exercise: Individual or group (if conducted collaboratively).

Materials needed:

- Access to academic literature for method selection and background research.
- Writing materials for drafting poems and documenting the research process.
- A classroom setting or group of participants for the study.

Activity:

Step 1: Identify a research question

Begin by observing your classroom environment. What interests you? What are the challenges? What themes emerge? As an example, you might find that students are having difficulty expressing their feelings about a particular topic or issue. Your research question could be: 'How can poetry help students express their feelings about topic X?'

Step 2: Choose a method

Review the methods mentioned in this section. Which one do you think would be the most effective for answering your research question? For instance, with the example research question in Step 1, poetic inquiry is likely to be the most suitable method as it allows students to express their thoughts and feelings through poetry.

Step 3: Design the study

Decide how you will apply the method. For example, with poetic inquiry, you might ask your students to author a poem about their feelings towards the chosen topic. Specify the length or style of the poem based on the classroom context and students' capabilities. Also, consider how you will gather the poems and analyse them. You may wish to devise a coding system or another form of qualitative analysis to identify common themes and sentiments.

Step 4: Ethical considerations

Consider how you will ensure the ethical treatment of your students' responses and poems, including getting ethical approval from your institution. You will need to make sure that students feel safe expressing their thoughts and emotions and that their work will be treated with respect. Explain the purpose of the study to them, ensuring their informed consent and the possibility to opt out if they wish. Their anonymity should be preserved unless they provide explicit consent to be identified.

Step 5: Conduct the study

Implement your plan. Ask students to draft their poems and remember to provide them with enough time and a supportive environment. You might even hold a special session or workshop to facilitate the poetry writing process.

Step 6: Analyse the data

Analyse the poems using your chosen method of analysis. Identify recurring themes, emotions, or other elements that stand out. These can provide rich insights into students' perspectives and feelings about the topic.

Step 7: Write up your findings

Summarise your process and findings in a write-up. Begin with an introduction that explains your research question and why you chose to use poetry as a method. Follow this with a detailed explanation of the method and the study design. Present your analysis, including the themes that emerged and any patterns you observed. Conclude by discussing what these findings mean for your research question, any limitations of the study, and potential avenues for future research.

Addressing challenges and finding solutions

As we explore the use of poetry in higher education research, we need to both celebrate the potentialities this innovative approach offers while preparing for the obstacles that may surface. It is these challenges and their resolutions that we shall turn our attention to in this section.

One of the foremost hurdles that researchers may grapple with is the initial unfamiliarity or discomfort with the language and techniques of poetry. Yet, proficiency in the poetic form is not a prerequisite for successful incorporation of poetry into research (Illingworth, 2022). Indeed, a willingness to experiment, learn, and grow is more important.

To mitigate this issue, researchers are encouraged to familiarise themselves with a broad range of poetic styles and forms. Reading widely can foster an understanding of how poets use language, imagery, and structure to convey meaning. Engaging in writing exercises and seeking constructive feedback can also enhance your comfort and skill with the poetic form (Alterio and McDrury, 2003). This is a continuous (and enjoyable) learning experience, and through every poetic reading, workshop, and encounter there is the opportunity as a researcher, educator, and human to discover new poetry and the lived experiences and worldviews that surround them.

Another challenge may stem from apprehension about the reception of research presented as poetry within the scholarly community. The academic sphere, with its traditionally analytical and empirical orientation, might appear daunting to those seeking to introduce a more emotive, qualitative dimension to their research.

However, as discussed in the Introduction, there is a growing recognition within academia of the value of diverse research methodologies. Researchers can draw on the increasing body of scholarly literature that validates and provides a theoretical basis for the use of poetry in research, including the case studies and research that have been presented in this chapter, and indeed throughout this book. Building a compelling rationale for your poetic approach, based on this literature and the specific objectives of the research, can strengthen the acceptance of this method.

One of the biggest criticisms that we often find levelled at us when using poetry in our own research is that it lacks validity and/or reliability as a research method, but this is simply not true.

Verifying the reliability and validity of a research method is crucial for establishing its trustworthiness. Reliability refers to the consistency of the measurements, while validity refers to the accuracy of measuring what is intended. When using poetry as a research method, reliability and validity can be verified as with any other qualitative research method (Golafshani, 2003).

Reliability can be ensured by comprehensive documentation throughout the research process. For example, if you were analysing a collection of poetry using thematic analysis, then this would mean including a detailed codebook and justifying each code and category. Such documentation allows the process to be explained to and repeated by others.

Likewise, validity can be established through strong auditing, justifying poetry selection and cleaning, and reporting this process. Providing rationale and contextualising with literature in the analysis also supports validity. For more on this topic, Korstjens and Moser (2018) offer some great guidance for assessing the trustworthiness of qualitative research, providing a detailed exploration of their meaning and application, particularly in studies incorporating content analysis.

We should also acknowledge the potential difficulty of maintaining integrity while transforming data into poetic form, as would be the case with poetic transcriptions or poetic autoethnographies. Striking a balance between artistic expression and fidelity to the data is a delicate task. Here, an ongoing reflective process is invaluable, with the need to confirm that the essence of the research is not lost in the poetic transformation.

A final challenge to consider is the potential for misunderstanding or misinterpretation that might arise due to the ambiguity inherent in poetry. Researchers can address this by providing a clear context for any poem that is used, explaining the research process and method, the intended meaning of the poem, and how this interpretation has arisen, including where appropriate an acknowledgment of the researcher(s) own positionality (Bourke, 2014). You might also encourage reader interaction, inviting interpretations and discussions that can enhance the understanding of the research.

To further illustrate how these challenges might be navigated, let us consider Kirsten's research into the experiences of compassion fatigue felt by undergraduate nursing students (Jack, 2017). Using an interpretative phenomenological approach, Kirsten analysed poetry written by first-year students, having provided them with a brief to write creatively about compassion. Kirsten selected poems which she interpreted as relating to compassion fatigue, based on her memories of distressing events from her own nursing education. Within the research, Kirsten makes her experiences clear, explicitly describing her positionality within the work. In doing so, she provides the reader with the lens through which she interprets the poetry, in the knowledge that the reader could interpret the poetry in a different way. Rather than viewing this as misunderstanding or misinterpretation, this method of analysis invites interaction from the reader and engages them in the whole process, which could lead to different outcomes, based on differing experiences.

In this research, Kirsten presented the student authored poems as written by them, without adding her interpretation to create something new. In contrast, Langer and Furman (2004), writing about experiences of identity, merged the participant's voice with the researcher's perspective, creating new poems from qualitative interview data. This method was helpful as it also afforded opportunities for the researcher's experience to be portrayed within the poems, something the authors suggest is often missed in qualitative research reporting. Such co-construction of the data, through poetry, fuses the researchers' insights with the participants' perspectives and can encourage researchers to examine and make more explicit their own position within the process (Leavy, 2020).

Further study

The Further study section in this chapter has been designed to provide practical opportunities to apply poetic research techniques in higher education contexts. Through analysing, transforming, synthesising, sculpting, and collaborating using poetry, these exercises should build your skills and generate insights to inform scholarly and pedagogical practice.

Analyse an existing poem. Select an existing poem that relates to a higher education topic or issue that interests you. This could be a published poem or one written by a student or colleague. Closely analyse the poem by asking questions such as: what is the main message or theme? What poetic techniques does the poet use? How does the poem portray the topic? What insights does the poem offer? Write a short reflection summarising your analysis and consider how this poem could inform your own higher education research project.

Transform an interview into a poem. Take an interview transcript you have from an existing research project. Select compelling excerpts and rearrange them into a poem. Aim to distil the key emotions and ideas from the interview into poetic form. When finished, reflect on how this process transformed the data and what insights emerge through this poetic representation.

Compose a found data poem. Gather textual data from your higher education environment, such as brochures, website content, bulletin board flyers, assignment guidelines, or marking rubrics. Select vivid phrases or statements from these sources to build a found poetry collage. Aim to creatively juxtapose different excerpts to generate new meanings and insights and write a reflection analysing what themes emerge in your found poetry collage.

Engage in poetic collaboration. Find one or two colleagues interested in using poetry as a research method. Have a 'poetic conversation' where you each create a short poem in response to each other's writings to generate an insightful dialogue. After a few rounds of exchange, reflect together on what new perspectives and understandings emerged from this collaboration. Discuss how this poetic process could be used as a research method.

Summary

As we close Chapter 4, we have illuminated how poetry can communicate complex ideas in accessible, emotive language, facilitating a deeper understanding of research findings.

We have also explored how poetry enhances the presentation of academic research, using a variety of case studies to demonstrate its tangible benefits. We also discussed some practical methods for incorporating poetry into research and examined solutions to potential challenges that might arise during this process.

As we look to the future of research in higher education, we encourage you to be innovative and bold, considering how poetry could enrich your own academic pursuits. We hope this chapter serves as an inspiration, empowering you to embrace this approach.

Now, as we turn to Chapter 5, we will pivot from research to introspection, exploring how poetry can be an invaluable tool for self-reflection in both learners and educators, deepening our understanding of ourselves and enhancing our educational journeys.

FIVE

Poetry for reflection

Chapter highlights

- Exploring the use of poetry to transform learning through reflection.
- Techniques for building poetic reflection in group discussions.
- Case studies showing the impact of poetic reflection in professional practice.
- Promoting reflective practice using poetry among colleagues.

Introduction

The aim of this chapter is to explore how poetry can be used to support personal and professional development, through experiential learning. We will consider how poetry enables reflection both in and on experiences in individual and group settings within higher education. Case studies and examples explore how poetry can be used to enhance critical thinking, emotional exploration, and creative evaluation of experience. Finally, we will consider how you might engage with poetry in your own experiential learning, to enable you to feel more comfortable when supporting this approach with other learners.

Engaging in reflective practice continues to be an important aspect for learners in higher education, in part because of the effect on personal and professional growth and development. Thinking reflectively is an active process in which we critically consider beliefs, knowledge, and action with a view to making future change (Dewey, 1933). Reflection can be both 'in action', taking place during an experience, or later, after the experience, when the event can be considered in the context of associated thoughts and feelings (Schön, 1991). Reflection can enable links between theory and practice, providing another way of learning, which engages the emotional aspects of development, making it a holistic way to learn from experiences. Understanding the link between the cognitive and affective aspects of learning can also support learners in making sense of events and enable a more critical exploration of experiences.

The need to reflect on practice is a regulatory requirement across several health professions such as nursing, medicine, and dentistry. However, the importance of learning through experience is not restricted to these groups and remains important across a range of areas such as law (Evans et al, 2017), veterinary practice, teacher education (Belvis et al, 2013), and for colleagues new to teaching in higher education (Smart, 2017). What we all have in common, and as highlighted by Schön (1991), is that there are some questions that can only be answered by actively thinking about our own experiences.

There are several reflective frameworks advocated to support learners to reflect on their experiences; for example, Gibbs (1988), Schön (1991) and Kolb (1984). While offering structure for learners, answering questions such as 'What were you thinking?' and 'What were you feeling?', can result in brief tick box answers, which might not encourage detailed discussions of the core of experiences and the associated meaning for the learner. The literature supports the notion that structured reflection, particularly through reflective templates, can be unpopular (Timmins et al, 2013; Campbell et al, 2022). It is not so much the framework itself, but the way in which it is interpreted, which can lead to learners viewing reflection as just another form to complete.

This exploration of poetry as a tool for reflection opens the door to a broader conversation about the adaptability of reflective practices in diverse educational settings, including online learning environments and larger group contexts. The challenges associated with traditional reflective frameworks, as highlighted by Timmins et al (2013) and Campbell et al (2022), are not confined to small, on-campus groups. These challenges are also prevalent in online learning spaces, where engagement can be more fragmented and impersonal. However, initiatives like Equity Unbound (Zamora et al, 2021), offer valuable insights into creating more inclusive and engaging reflective experiences. By fostering an environment where every learner feels valued and heard, regardless of the size or nature of the learning space, reflective practices can be more meaningful and impactful.

Incorporating these principles into reflective activities can transform the way learners interact with and understand their experiences. For instance, in large online classes, structured reflection through poetry can provide a more personal and in-depth exploration of learning experiences. This approach not only encourages deeper engagement but also helps in bridging the gap often felt in virtual learning environments. By allowing for diverse modes of expression and ensuring that all voices are equally heard, educators can create a more equitable and inclusive space for reflection. This aligns with the findings of Bali and Zamora (2023), who advocate for an approach where community building is not just about welcoming ideas but actively nurturing and valuing them. Such an approach to reflective learning can be particularly powerful in large groups and online settings, where the risk of disconnection and superficial engagement is higher.

How poetry transforms learning from experience

Several authors (including both Sam and Kirsten) have embraced poetry as a different way to support reflection, across numerous disciplines (Day, 2018; Jack and Illingworth, 2019; Matthews, 2022; Whittle et al, 2022). Indeed, Wakeman (2013) suggests poetry is especially helpful to capture experience due to the way it engages the imagination, cognition, and linguistic capacities, to both articulate and document events. Wakeman (2013, p 187) identifies the impact of writing poetry in experiential writing, in that it can: 'freeze and portray the colour, emotion, or delight of an experience, and make it available to the writer later, so that rich memories come flooding back, or other readers can enter into the experience'.

Poems are unusual, in that they do not normally present us with facts. This makes a refreshing change in contrast to the amount of information with which we bombard learners daily in higher education institutions. Instead, poetry explores the hard-to-reach core of what it means to be human, enabling us to develop a sense of what gives value and shape to our lives (Shapiro, 2010). In doing so, poems enable us to recognise aspects of ourselves we might have forgotten, often leading to new perspectives on old situations and the healing of longstanding wounds. Ultimately, this leads to a more meaningful reflective experience for both us and our learners.

Stageberg and Anderson (1952) summarise this hard to capture experience, which happens within us when we read words in a poem. For them, this experience of reading and feeling *is* the poem; a response determined by both the nature of our past experiences with the words on the page, and our current emotional state of mind. This experience is why poetry is so helpful for reflective practice, as the connection made will differ between each learner and further, might be different from one day to the next, depending on changes in daily feelings. This unique and personal resonance with poetry can make us feel understood, as if the poet has insight into our experiences. This makes poetry a powerful tool for reflective practice. This magical connection is far removed from the rigid reflective templates we expect our learners to complete and can lead to transformative learning taking place as they become more self-accepting, and less challenged by the prospect of change and growth.

Speaking from a medical education perspective, Whittle et al (2022) suggests that engaging with creative methods is helpful to promote reflection on practice, with poetry identified as offering specific advantages and further opportunities for deeper reflexivity. Reflexivity is an element of reflection which is when we explore ways to question our own attitudes, values, assumptions, and habits, to help us understand how we relate to others (Bolton, 2014). When we are reflexive, we question 'from within experiences', a complex and dynamic process leading to growth and development, as we stand back and look at ourselves from the outside in. Poetry supports a deepening of this reflexive process in several ways: through group discussion, through the development of empathy via perspective transformation, and through the language of poetry itself (Whittle et al, 2022).

As an example, here is a reflective poem written by Sam, about one of his most formative learning experiences: taken from when he was a Lecturer at Manchester Metropolitan University.

In his first ever lecture, Sam waited outside the classroom to shake hands with the cohort. One of the female students said she could not shake his hand for cultural reasons. Sam felt incredibly embarrassed and worried that he had upset, shamed, or offended the student, and wrote the following poem to reflect on this experience:

Aligning Our Needs

In my first lecture
I waited outside
the classroom
to shake hands.
One of the students said

she could not.
I felt embarrassed
for a shame
we shared.

By rendering his recollection into poetic form, Sam was able to achieve a deeper level of introspection about this formative incident. The act of consciously selecting each word forced him to distil the essence of the interaction and confront his own lapses in cultural awareness. Beyond examining this single occurrence, the poetic reflection enabled him to consider his broader pedagogical philosophy and positionality as an educator. Sam realised that while his intention to connect personally with students was admirable, he needed greater sensitivity regarding diverse backgrounds and sensibilities. The insight gleaned from this reflective process underscored the importance of open communication, empathy, and flexibility when working to align his methods with the needs of individual learners. Sam emerged with a renewed commitment to fostering an inclusive educational environment where all students feel recognised, valued, and empowered to thrive academically on their own terms. You will also be relieved to read that he also no longer waits outside lecture theatres waiting to shake the hands of his students.

Building poetic reflection though group discussion

Smart (2017) explores how although much is made of learning from experience in higher education, the reflective process itself will usually be limited, as it is normally an individual endeavour, rarely involving others. This can be beneficial, enabling learners to write, free from another's judgement, although it often leaves them with only their own perspective to consider.

Writing from the perspective of an academic developer, Smart (2014) introduced the concept of 'poetic transcription with a twist'. This innovative approach, building upon the research method of poetic transcription discussed in Chapter 4, places reflection within a group setting. It involves individuals sharing a story from their experience, typically a 'critical incident', and then retelling it in poetic form both individually and with contributions from other group members. This developmental process turns not only the storyteller but also their peers into poets, fostering a collaborative learning environment. Smart and Loads (2017) emphasise the significance of this method in mitigating feelings of isolation, as it encourages sharing and learning from each other's experiences.

Group collaboration in poetic reflection, as Jack and Illingworth (2019) suggest, requires adept facilitation, offering opportunities for both the facilitator and the students to grow mutually. Any critical incident chosen for these reflections is often an event that went awry or led to an undesirable outcome, but as Smart and Loads (2017) note, the process of sharing these experiences in a supportive, non-judgemental atmosphere can also become an occasion to acknowledge and celebrate successes. Campo (2020) underscores the impact of such shared experiences: the simple act of being present with others during these reflective sessions can foster joy and resilience, offering a buffer against burnout and stress. This highlights the power of communal reflection in an academic setting, where the shared act of poetic expression can lead to a deeper, more meaningful learning experience.

Developing empathy

Shapiro et al (2006b) suggest there are several relationships between all steps of the creative writing, reading, and listening process and the development of empathy. Empathy is important as an interpersonal competence described by the phenomenologist Edith Stein as a feeling-based *experience* of another person's feeling (Svenaeus, 2018). To develop such a complex capability requires us to feel uncertain and delay making assumptions about how others might be feeling. The ambiguous nature of poetry can often leave us with more questions than answers and because of this, we are forced to consider voices other than our own and be open to several different worldviews (Chavis, 2011).

This provides opportunities for the rehearsal of empathy, developed through listening to poetry written by others (Jack and Illingworth, 2023). However, reflection on our own poetry gives us another empathic opportunity, which is the development of *self*-empathy. This is an important aspect of self-care not only for our learners but also educators, as we navigate the often-stressful environments of higher education. The concept of self-empathy is less well known than the empathy we show to others, although it can lead to a kinder self-assessment of our actions, leading to shifts in perspective (Sherman, 2014). There are also opportunities for reflexivity here, as we view ourselves as two separate entities through our poetry. This enables access to emotions about events within our writing, but viewing them in a less judgemental way, as we objectively look in on ourselves from the outside.

Using published poetry, which is particularly ambiguous or written from different perspectives, can also be helpful to explore empathy and promote further reflective writing. For example, Kirsten has used the poem 'Health Check' by Penny Feinstein (2007) to challenge stereotypical views of ageing and the ways health professionals communicate with older people. The following lines from this poem enable reflection on the difference between what we might say to another person and what they might hear:

> 'Life choices' you coo,
> but I hear '*One hundred lines*
> *to be written in your lunch hour*'

Poems can offer uncertainty, which can be troubling for learners, but also provide opportunities for self-growth and exploration and engagement in a deep reflexive process. Another example of an ambiguous poem, often used in a therapeutic setting is 'The Road Not Taken', by Robert

Frost (1916). When hearing the last two lines, some perceive a positive choice, whereas others hear regret (Chavis, 2011):

> I took the road less travelled by,
> and that has made all the difference.

Poems like this can spark meaningful reflection, as learners explore decisions they have taken and alternative choices they might have made, through insightful exploration.

How poetic reflection shifts perspectives

We have discussed the benefits of using poetry to reflect, in terms of building collaborative spaces and supporting empathy development to both ourselves and others. Poetry also offers us opportunities to engage in perspectival shifts on situations, as we are given opportunities to revisit events, and the feelings that surround them. As discussed, using poems such as 'Health Check' and 'The Road Not Taken' can bring another poetic voice into the reflective discussion. Group reflection combines several perspectives from peers in the collaborative process which might lead to a kinder re-evaluation of events for the learner who provided the incident. As Meehan (2002) suggests, revisiting what we thought we already knew enables a deeper understanding and such circular motion enables us to revisit each time from a fresh perspective.

Specific poems can be helpful in this perspectival shifting process, leading to greater self-discovery and ultimate acceptance of who we are. For example, Robert Frost's poem, 'The Armful' (Frost, 1928), describes the dropping and picking up of parcels and can resonate with the challenges faced by learners, such as time management and meeting deadlines. Exploring these issues using imagery helps learners to recognise these challenges in an indirect way, potentially enabling a more compassionate response. Frost's poem is empathic in tone, signalling the need for a more helpful arrangement of the 'parcels', using the lines:

I had to drop the armful in the road.
And try to stack them in a better load.

There are opportunities within this poem for discussions emphasising the need to prioritise and consider the importance of self-care. Another poem which could be used alongside The Armful, is 'Snowbound', by Natasha Lynne Vogdes (1980).[1] Writing in a therapeutic context, Chavis (2011) describes how the imagery of this poem can be helpful when working alongside people who might have difficulty in saying no. This can be true of our learners, who might prioritise the needs of others over their own. For example, the following lines can enable discussion of how we perceive our own needs in relation to those of others, potentially leading to perspective shifts in relation to our own self-care:

There is time to stop travelling …
    to get off other people's subways
    to halt airplanes from landing in your life.
A time to refuel yourself.

Poems can act as a springboard for both you and your learners to explore your own feelings about situations at a more meaningful reflective level. Taking lines that 'speak' to you can prompt your own poetry writing and unearth perspectives that might even be hidden from yourself until you start to write. Kirsten was inspired to write a piece of poetic reflection after reading these lines from Vogdes' poem to re-examine and more deeply understand habits which she needed to review with fresh eyes. Continuing the theme of planes, she wrote the following:

So Many Airplanes

So many airplanes
landing on the runway
of my life, leaving marks.

Those big black tyres, scars of my
failure, to say no.

I am thrown to the side,
or should I say, I let them,
push me.
My brain incapable of
stopping the big red beating thing in
my chest, which weighs in.

I know better! it says,
in its bullying style.
Like a super heavyweight boxer,
pumping over reason.
It will never learn, here it
comes again.

They have a bad relationship.
The stairs between the two
are like a cartoon.
Full of wood worm which
will never be treated.

EXERCISE 5.1: POETRY AS A SPRINGBOARD FOR REFLECTION

Estimated engagement time: 60–90 minutes.

Aim: To facilitate a deep self-reflection using poetry as a catalyst.

Objectives:

- To engage with poetry on a personal level, identifying lines or phrases that resonate.
- To generate a personal poetic reflection, fostering self-awareness and emotional articulation.

Output: A reflective poem and a deeper personal understanding of a chosen theme or emotion.

Type of exercise: Individual.

Materials needed:

- A selection of meaningful poems.
- Writing materials or a digital device for documenting reflections.

Activity:

Step 1: Read a poem that speaks to you

At this point in the book, you should have identified several poems that are meaningful for you or chosen some for your teaching. Select one of these, or one discussed in this chapter, and read it a few times aloud.

Step 2: Find your meaningful springboard

Having read the poem a few times, locate the line which holds the most meaning for you at this time. It might feel like this line is sucking you in, as if the writer has written this with an understanding of you, and where you are in your life at this time. Alternatively, you might not be able to explain *why* this line is important to you. Perhaps it just speaks to you, but you are uncertain about the reason.

Step 3: Use the line to start your own poetic reflection

In the example just discussed, Kirsten used the lines about landing airplanes, to explore her feelings about habits she had developed, which left her feeling worn down and in need of more self-care. Now take your line, or words, and without thinking too much about it, start to free write your own reflective poem. Do not pay any attention to grammar or spelling, just write for about 5 minutes.

Step 4: Review your poetic reflection

Now read your reflective poem. Are you surprised about what you wrote? Which aspect of the experience was most meaningful for you? You can now put your reflection away or perhaps you want to work more on your poem, to explore more deeply, your thoughts and feelings on the focus of your writing.

Specific poetic language to support reflection

Metaphors might be considered a 'figure of speech', enabling a connection between our 'internal and external reality' (Mazza,

2022; p 23). Similarly, Furman (2004) suggests metaphors are essential in poetry writing and have a far greater impact than merely describing an event as it happened, as might happen using reflective templates. Metaphors enable writers to pack far more feeling into their writing, as they enable the making of comparisons without being explicit, which makes for more powerful writing. For example, saying 'My life is like a war zone', is not quite as impactful as the line, 'My life *is* a war zone'. Further, metaphorical writing is particularly helpful during the reflective process, as it enables writers to articulate things they might not yet properly understand.

Metaphors have the potential to move us further on in our reflections, beyond the obvious, and in doing so, open new possibilities for understanding both the self and others (Hiley, 2006). Metaphorical language supports the development of intuitive knowing, enabling learners to go beyond the cognitive rational mind and find a wider meaning to events (Fox, 1997). Our own research with nursing students suggests the ability to use metaphor in reflective poetry enables the exploration of emotion in ways that enable some distance between the event under discussion and its exploration (Jack and Illingworth, 2017). For example, learners might feel reluctant to talk directly about how they feel, so saying, 'I am a dull and rainy day' might be easier than stating that they are sad, distressed, or unhappy. Combs and Freedman (1990) also discuss how emotions can be explored through symbol and metaphor; for example, describing the feeling as an image, action, sound, or film star. One way to encourage learners to do this could be to ask them to write a list poem (see Exercise 2.3), about their feelings and another one about items found in the kitchen and then task them with writing a poetic reflection about one of the listed feelings as one of the listed items.

Another idea which could support reflective poetry writing using metaphorical language is by using a 'then and now' framework. Chavis (2011) cites an anonymous poem which employs this structure, using the words 'I used to be …' to introduce the first stanza. This is followed by, 'Now I am …', which is used to begin stanza two. Facilitators can decide the category of metaphor, for example, colours, cities, buildings, or foods. Here are two examples of this framework in action, written by Kirsten and Sam, respectively, using foods to explore self-knowledge, change, and growth.

Kirsten's poem

I used to be pizza.

Piled high,
with energy.
A mix of random,
until it didn't work.
A bit like the Hawaiian one.
I used to be pulled.
Different ways,
no sense to it.
What will I be today?
A bit like the balls,
in those games,
my brothers used to play.

Now I am flan.

Smoother, softer edged,
Still bouncy, like the balls,
but less scratchy on the mouth.
I slide more,
pulled less.

Sam's poem

I used to be coffee.
Bitter and bold,
jolting the senses

with caffeinated fervour.
Dark roasted intensity and
steaming hot takes
poured out compulsively –
opinions percolating,
seeking to stir and invigorate.

Now I am honey.
Sucrose susurrations.
still strong but
flowing,
not forcing.
Sticking,
not scalding.
The same richness
distilled
into purer purpose –
to nourish,
not needle.

EXERCISE 5.2: WRITING YOUR OWN 'THEN AND NOW' POEM

Estimated engagement time: 30 minutes.

Aim: To facilitate a deep self-reflection using poetry as a catalyst.

Objectives:

- To engage with poetry on a personal level, identifying lines or phrases that resonate.
- To generate a personal poetic reflection, fostering self-awareness and emotional articulation.

Output: A reflective poem and a deeper personal understanding of a chosen theme or emotion.

Type of exercise: Individual.

Materials needed:

- A selection of meaningful poems.
- Writing materials or a digital device for documenting reflections.

Activity:

Step 1: Choose your favourite category of metaphor

Decide on your metaphor but do not take too long over this. Pick something that pops into your head without too much deliberation.

Step 2: Write using the 'I used to be, Now I am' stems

Taking your metaphor as a guide, write your reflective poem for about 5 minutes. As with Exercise 5.1, do not pay too much attention to spelling or grammar at this stage.

Step 3: Review your reflective poem

Now read back what you have written. How playful were you in your poem? Did you uncover more metaphors? You can either keep your poem somewhere safe, or continue to work on it, as you uncover your thoughts and feelings, perhaps in a metaphorical way. You might now also want to use this experience to develop a similar exercise for your learners.

Case studies

We will now explore a selection of case studies, which develop our understanding of how poetry can be used to enhance reflective practice in higher education. We have chosen examples of both group and individual reflection, and published and self-authored poetry, across several contexts.

Case study 5.1: Reflecting on nursing practice

Key takeaway: Offers insights into how poetry can be a reflective tool for nursing students to process their clinical experiences and foster community through shared narratives.

The first case study, drawn from a qualitative study written by Kirsten and Sam, offers insight into the perspectives of both undergraduate nursing students and their educators on the process of writing poetry to reflect on experience (Jack and Illingworth, 2019). This study was developed from an innovative pedagogical project, which included the development of an online repository, designed to support the sharing of student poetry to connect them with their peers.

All students were invited to write poems about their clinical practice, following their first clinical placement experience. The first placement can often be a challenging experience for students, as they become exposed to the reality of nursing, which might not always be what they expected, leading to a readjustment of expectations. Students were subsequently asked to share their poems in small groups of about 10–15 peers, supported by an educator. All educators were supported to facilitate these sessions through preparatory discussions and proper scaffolding (see Chapter 2).

This study identified several important findings, following unstructured qualitative interviews with students and educators involved in the reflections. First was the freedom afforded by the invitation to write poems in contrast to the restriction of reflective templates. Permitted more freedom, learners were able to explore nursing more holistically, acknowledging diversity both in the people they care for and within themselves.

Importantly, both the learner and educator participants agreed poetry writing could have a beneficial effect on clinical practice, through supporting the development of empathy and self-awareness. This study found that when learners listen to the poetry written by their peers, their empathic abilities grow, as they take the opportunity to listen to diverse perspectives. Even students who might not be willing to share what they have written benefit from hearing the experiences, emotions, and thoughts of their peers, thereby reducing their own feelings of isolation.

Case study 5.2: Reflecting in general practice registrar education

Key takeaway: Reveals how sharing and discussing poetry can provide emotional expression and peer support in educational environments that may not typically encourage such openness.

This case study was conducted by William Foster and Elaine Freeman (2008) and was focused on exploring how poetry can support learners to express feelings in a culture that does not always support this behaviour. It provides a contrast in method to our first case study, in that both facilitators and learners chose published poetry to share with their peers for discussion, rather than being asked to write their own poems.

Learners were divided into two groups and each experienced two 1-hour sessions, 1 week apart. The first session used facilitator-selected poetry and in the second, the learners were asked to contribute their own choices. Simple advice was given to the learners about poem choice, essentially requesting work which appealed to them. For the facilitators, criteria for poem choice included work that was not too lengthy or well known, was easy to read aloud, was revealing of human experience, and had some ambiguity.

Interviews, using an interpretative phenomenological approach, revealed several important findings in relation to reflective practice. These poetry sessions enabled the learners to explore the emotional aspects of their medical practice, allowing consideration of both their own and other's humanity. The ambiguity inherent within the poetry also enabled them to practice their skills of perception, inviting them to try to understand another person's perspective and thereby their response to the needs of others.

Learners involved in these sessions had previously reported difficulty in the expression of their emotions within the medical culture. These poetry sessions were effective in providing an environment for emotional exploration and the development of empathy both to themselves and others. Learners were able to see how through engagement with poetry, they developed skills of close reading, listening, and interpretation, all helpful when needing to understand an individual's unique illness experience and for the promotion of holistic person-centred care.

There is some important learning from this study when planning poetry related reflective sessions for our own learners. The authors suggest that when the learners chose their own poetry to share with the group, they were more likely to express their emotions and reveal personal insights. Further, by bringing in poems on the day, there was a need for spontaneous facilitation, which enabled group leadership to be shared, as participants and facilitators were on a more equal level, creating further opportunities for agency and empowerment.

Case study 5.3: Reflecting on counselling practice

Key takeaway: Examines the therapeutic role of poetry in personal and professional growth, demonstrating poetry's value in reflective and expressive writing for counsellors.

The final case study is from Jeannie Wright (2003) and involves the use of expressive writing for self-discovery and personal and professional growth. Wright explores her experiences of reflection from a personal rather than academic angle, wanting her own story to be heard to evoke a different response in the reader. We have included this work here as it provides an example of how the author wrote poetry as a form of private exploration, not initially written to be shared with others. The author employs poetry to process startling client stories professionally and to navigate personal events, such as her father's death.

Wright's example highlights the question of who and what reflective writing is for. Reflection is personal, a place for us to explore our thoughts, feelings, and experiences in a place where we will not be judged, and for Wright it was about 'protection and survival' (p 197). However, professional requirements and university learning outcomes often lead to reflective writing being assessed, thereby inhibiting the freedom of expression we want so much to encourage. As Wright suggests, it is ironic that she was fearful about verbally sharing her emotions, considering her background in talking therapies. However, her fear was lessened as she was in control of her writing, treating it as something she could keep private until she chose to share it.

There are parallels between Wright's experiences and those of our learners, in that many might feel anxious about revealing too much of themselves through the sharing of their own poetic reflections, or the emotions evoked when reading the poetry of others. However, encouraging students to write poetry as regular reflections on their personal and professional lives can support their development in emotional exploration via the provision of a non-judgemental space in which to engage in self-growth.

EXERCISE 5.3: PLANNING A REFLECTIVE ACTIVITY FOR YOUR LEARNERS

Estimated engagement time: 45–60 minutes.

Aim: To design a reflective activity using poetry to support students in exploring personal and/or professional themes.

Objectives:

- Identify a clear focus for the reflective activity aligned with learning outcomes.
- Choose a suitable method for facilitating reflective practice through poetry.
- Plan for the evaluation of the activity to inform future teaching practices.

Output: A detailed plan for a reflective poetic activity tailored to your learners' needs and your educational objectives.

Type of exercise: Individual planning.

Materials needed:

- Case studies from this chapter.
- Writing materials or a digital device for planning.
- Any additional resources based on the chosen method for the activity (for example published poetry, examples of reflective poems, and so on).

Activity:

Step 1: Identify a focus

Consider your goals and what you want to achieve. For example, is this a new group of learners who you want to know better through their reflective pieces? Or do you want to explore an aspect of professional development through reflective writing? Having a focus is also helpful for learners to channel their reflective explorations in contrast to an unstructured approach, which might lead them unwittingly to exploring uncomfortable territory.

Step 2: Choose a method

Review the case studies in this chapter. We explored several methods, each helpful for students to encourage reflective practice. Thinking about the aim and focus of the reflection, which one do you think would be most helpful? For example, do you want to adopt Foster and Freeman's (2008) ideas and ask students to bring in published poetry on a particular topic for group discussion? Or perhaps you are considering inviting students to write their own poems, at a certain point in time, like the undergraduate nurses in Jack and Illingworth's (2019) study.

Step 3: Group or individual reflections

Consider whether you will be asking students to develop group reflections or inviting individual pieces. You might encourage students to work together, sharing their perspectives within one creative piece. Alternatively, you might invite individual pieces; for example, adopting the 'then and now' framework discussed previously, to share self-growth and development.

Step 4: Evaluate the activity

As with all educational interventions, evaluating how it went is helpful for you as an educator to support your own growth and development. Reflection is personal and assessing how well it 'worked' can be problematic. Not least because learners might only realise the power of the activity some hours, days or months later. To effectively gauge the impact, consider implementing follow-up sessions or feedback mechanisms at a later stage, allowing students to share their retrospective insights and experiences.

Promoting poetic reflection with colleagues

The essence of creative reflection for practitioners lies in its ability to meld research and practice through a comprehensive, imaginative lens. It propels a deeper understanding and engagement with one's craft, be it solitary or collaborative, traditional or digitally mediated, highlighting how reflective creative mindsets can unveil new insights and challenges (Candy, 2019). In this chapter, we have explored how we might develop collaborative reflective communities for our learners to support meaningful reflection, although we can readily apply such examples to ourselves, in support of our own development. Johns (2010) describes how we often lose touch with our imagination, and with it, our creativity and intuition. In our professional lives, we are expected to be rational, which leads to a stunting of our creativity. Johns (2010) also suggests poetry takes us further than description, to capture the meaning of experiences; a way to deepen our thinking is to take some writing then craft it into a poem. This process is like the blackout poetry discussed in the case studies of Chapter 2, although here we can use lines of our reflective writing to create a poem. Such poems move us into a more reflective way of being and can help to home in on feelings as new images arise through our imagination (Johns, 2010).

We can then share these newly formed poetic reflections with others, potentially discussing them in groups, to develop a reflective thinking space. We can also make published poetry part of our everyday lives, through reading more of it or perhaps listening to the poems of other educators and facilitators. Podcasts such as 'The Poetry Exchange' celebrate poems 'as friends' by inviting guests to discuss poems that have meaning to them. This is an excellent way for you to expose yourself to new poems, that you perhaps would not have normally discovered, and which you can then share with others, perhaps to enable some group reflection.

For example, Kirsten often shares 'A Gift' by Denise Levertov (1996) with other academics to act as a basis for reflection on teaching in higher education. The poem ends ambiguously, providing opportunities for reflection on what it means and how it might relate to our own emotional way of being:

> You are given the questions of others
> as if they were answers
> to all you ask. Yes, perhaps
> this gift is your answer.[2]

The business of life as an academic can sometimes remove us from the very reasons we entered a career in teaching in the first place, and in this instance, using this poem for group reflection raises themes around nurturing, sharing knowledge, and the often hard-to-capture gifts we share with learners, which might go unrecognised by both them and us.

Further study

The Further study section in this chapter has been designed to provide practical opportunities to apply poetic techniques to enhance reflective practice in higher education contexts. Through analysing, transforming, synthesising, and collaborating, these exercises aim to build your skills and generate insights to inform reflective learning with educators and learners alike.

Analyse a reflective poem about teaching. Select an existing reflective poem about teaching or education. Consider how the poem offers insights into the teaching experience. Write a reflection summarising what the poem reveals about the emotional dimensions of teaching and how it could inform your own reflective teaching practice.

Transform a teaching observation into a poem. Take notes from observing a colleague. Select compelling excerpts and rearrange them into a reflective poem from the educator's perspective. Aim to distil their experience into poetic form and reflect on how this poetic transformation enhances empathy and understanding of your own teaching practice.

Compose a found reflection poem on mentoring. Gather artifacts related to mentoring students, like emails, notes, or journal entries. Select vivid phrases describing meaningful moments in these mentoring relationships. Rearrange them into a poetic reflection capturing the essence of mentoring, and in doing so consider what the poem reveals about fostering student growth.

Engage students in collaborative poetic reflection. Have students reflect on a meaningful learning experience by collaboratively writing a poem together. Invite them to contribute phrases and lines to co-construct a poem synthesising their shared insights. After composing the communal reflection, invite discussion around what new perspectives emerged from this poetic approach.

Summary

As we end this chapter, it is time to consider how poetry can be used to breathe new life into our own reflective practices and those of our learners. We have seen how poetry can trigger our imagination, enable fresh perspectives to emerge, and bring us closer to knowing who we are and what we stand for in higher education and beyond.

We have explored the different ways poetry can be used to deepen our experiential learning, providing case studies and examples that explore several ways that poetry can be used to reflect, be that alone or in groups of supportive colleagues. Poetry, either published or self-authored, can support our reflection in new ways, leading to self-learning, development, and personal and professional growth.

As we progress into Chapter 6, we encourage you to use some of the examples in this chapter to reflect on your journey to date, considering how the integration of poetry into the fabric of your practice has enriched the work you do. We invite you to consider how you might continue to develop your reflection using poetic methods to foster imagination and intuition, and how you can share your new knowledge with others.

SIX

Epilogue

Chapter highlights

- Reflecting on the journey of integrating poetry in higher education.
- Evaluating the impact of poetic practices and adjusting approaches.
- Strategies for sustaining momentum and future directions for poetry in education.
- Final reflections on the transformative power of poetry in academia.

Introduction

We have now reached the final stop on our journey exploring the dynamic role poetry can play in higher education. Across the chapters of this book, we have traversed diverse yet interconnected territories, guided by a shared vision of poetry's transformative potential. From nurturing creativity in teaching to capturing nuances in research, we have attempted to shine a light on the multiple ways in which poetry can enrich learning and growth.

In Chapter 1, we set out to challenge the traditional parameters of academia characterised by speed, performativity, and standardisation by illuminating the transformative potential of poetry within higher education. Through the subsequent chapters, we explored this landscape, highlighting poetry's capacity to stimulate creativity in the classroom, facilitate authentic assessments, conduct research, and nourish personal growth. In doing so we aimed to firmly establish poetry as an invaluable instrument that is both academically rigorous and deeply humanising.

This concluding chapter provides an opportunity to reflect on our travels. We will look back on what was discussed, distilling pivotal insights revealed along the way. We will also look ahead with optimism, considering how poetry may continue to evolve within higher education in the future. Our aim is to provide guidance and inspiration as you start to chart your own course, sustaining this momentum in your individual contexts within higher education.

Primarily, we wish to emphasise that this poetic journey is not one with a defined end point. Rather, it is an open-ended, lifelong process of discovery. Our intention throughout this book was not to present poetry as a rigid set of techniques, but rather as a wellspring of creative possibilities within teaching, learning, research, and reflection. We aimed to spark curiosity and empower experimentation, to enrich educational practices with sentiment, artistry, and humanity.

The heart of our message is a belief in poetry's capacity to engender perspectives, empower voices, and discover meanings. We have explored how poetry provides insights into diverse lived experiences, builds emotional intelligence, and nurtures empathy. Across disciplines and environments, poetry yields an enriched understanding of ourselves, our students, and higher education itself.

In the classroom context, we have discussed how poetry facilitates interactive, imaginative learning. Whether using found poetry to synthesise concepts or crafting communal poems to explore shared experiences, poetic approaches were shown to stimulate creativity, critical thinking, and connection. For educators, we strongly believe that incorporating poetry also enables more authentic, open-ended teaching, embracing vulnerability to enhance rapport with our learners.

Poetry likewise offers exciting possibilities for assessment and feedback. For example, the constraints of crafting a poem compel learners to extract knowledge, communicating insights with creativity. This provides a novel form of authentic assessment where students can display genuine understanding. Poetry can also add humanity and imagination to feedback, evoking emotion alongside analysis.

We have also investigated poetry as a research methodology within higher education. The use of poetic inquiry, transcription, and autoethnography provides nuance and depth that can be absent in more conventional methods. Poetry communicates scholarly insights evocatively, bringing to life the complex human experiences at the heart of higher education research. This expands possibilities for innovation within our classrooms and beyond.

Additionally, we have explored how poetry facilitates reflection for both students and educators. Poetic writing and reading fosters self-awareness, enables processing of experiences, and nurtures growth (Quinlan, 2016). Engaging with poetry develops intrapersonal and interpersonal intelligence, empowering more contemplative, empathetic practice for both educators and learners alike.

Woven through these discussions has been a shared ethos valuing creativity, diversity, and compassion within education. We believe poetry provides openings to humanise academic practices often constrained by conformity, competition, and hierarchy. The expressiveness and subjectivity of poetry offers a conduit for plurality and purposeful learning.

Of course, integrating poetry into higher education comes with inherent challenges. Student and teacher discomfort, perceptions of irrelevance, limitations of assessment, and scarcity of exemplars require acknowledgement. We aimed to confront these barriers directly, providing advice to implement poetic techniques in a gradual, scaffolded manner. Critically, we believe that the benefits of enriched perspective and deeper learning outweigh the necessary growing pains of innovation.

As your individual contexts also shape these poetic possibilities, we encourage you to adapt, experiment, and evolve. There is no perfect formula, only the expansive potential of poetry when interwoven into teaching, learning, research, and reflection. We hope this book has sparked new interest in exploring that potential within your own practice.

Moving forward, sustaining the momentum of this endeavour will be crucial, as will nurturing communities to collaboratively elevate the role of poetry in higher education. Although pockets of interest exist, a systemic shift remains gradual. Realising poetry's far-reaching benefits demands our continued action across institutions and environments. This concluding chapter offers guidance for reflecting on your efforts thus far and planning future poetic integration.

Fundamentally, we envision a future where poetry is woven into the fabric of higher education. Where lively poetic perspectives routinely energise teaching, learning, research, and growth. Wherever your own path may lead, we hope poetry remains close, whispering inspiration, offering insight, and deepening your educational experiences.

Reflecting on your poetic journey

Having explored the possibilities of poetry across diverse educational contexts, it is now apt to pause and reflect on your own poetic journey in higher education thus far. What initially motivated you to engage with poetry? Why did you pick up this book? Have you tried out any of the exercises we have provided? How have your experiments integrating any of these poetic techniques progressed? What challenges, insights, and revelations have you encountered along the way?

In Chapter 1, you completed two key exercises to ignite your exploration of poetry's potential in higher education, Exercise 1.1: Exploring your relationship with poetry, and Exercise 1.2: Challenges in your field. Now that you have progressed through this book, reflecting on those initial exercises can provide valuable perspective on your growth.

EXERCISE 6.1: REFLECTING ON YOUR POETIC JOURNEY

Estimated engagement time: 30–45 minutes.

Aim: To reflect on your poetic journey throughout the course and evaluate how your perception and application of poetry in higher education has evolved.

Objectives:

- Revisit initial exercises to assess growth and evolving perspectives on poetry.
- Reflect on experiences and learning throughout the book.
- Set actionable goals for continued exploration and integration of poetry in higher education practice.

Output: A reflective piece outlining your poetic journey, evolved insights, and future goals regarding the incorporation of poetry in your educational practice.

Type of exercise: Individual reflection.

Materials needed:

- Notes and reflections from Exercises 1.1 and 1.2.
- Writing materials or a digital device for reflection and goal setting.

Activity:

Step 1: Revisit Exercise 1.1

Review your notes from Exercise 1.1 where you reflected on meaningful encounters with poetry. How has your appreciation for and relationship with poetry expanded since then based on what you have learned? Are you engaging with poetry in new ways personally or professionally?

Step 2: Revisit Exercise 1.2

Read the discipline-specific challenges you identified in Exercise 1.2. Have your views on how poetry might help address those challenges shifted or been strengthened? Are there new possibilities you now see for leveraging poetry?

Step 3: Assess your growth

Reflect holistically on how your understanding of and openness to poetry has grown over the course of reading and working through this book. What stands out as most influential or surprising? How has it changed how you view the potential of poetry in your own context?

Step 4: Set future goals

Based on your reflections, write down two or three specific goals for continuing to build poetry into your higher education practice in the future, whether teaching, research, assessment, or personal growth. This lays the foundation for sustaining your momentum.

Evaluating impact and adjusting approaches

Following mindful reflection, the next phase is to evaluate the impact of poetic techniques implemented thus far, using this to strengthen future efforts and counter potential dissenters or opposition to this approach. As with any pedagogical innovation, you need to analyse poetry's effects on key outcomes and be responsive to areas that need refinement (Walder, 2017). This enables us as educators to continually adjust our approach, improving poetry's integration in the process.

Evaluating the effect of poetic techniques and adjusting our approaches accordingly are key to strengthening poetry's integration in higher education. As with any other approach to learning and teaching in higher education, you should gather data, analyse effects on learning, and reflect on what went well, what could be improved in the future, and what learning and transformation has taken place for you personally. Here are some recommended methods for doing so:

- **Surveys.** Develop pre- and post-surveys asking learners to rate poetry's influence on their motivation, enjoyment, creativity, retention, comprehension, critical thinking, and other key attributes. Include open-ended questions for qualitative insights into what poetic approaches worked best and why, potentially giving learners the opportunity to respond poetically. Recognise that poetry's impacts may take time to fully emerge, so also consider longitudinal data collection at later points, interviews, or reflective journals to capture longer-term perspectives on how learners' skills developed through poetry. The evolving and multilayered nature of poetry means its effects are not always immediately quantifiable, so employ a range of qualitative and quantitative measures over time to gain a fuller picture of learners' growth.
- **Interviews/focus groups.** Conduct interviews or focus groups with a diverse sample of learners and other educators to gather in-depth perspectives. Explore their perceptions of poetry's benefits and limitations, including factors like its impact on reflection, empathy, engagement with the subject matter, and suggestions for improving how it is incorporated into any of your materials.
- **Analysis of student artifacts.** Reviewing key student assessments (both formative and summative) before and after the introduction of poetic techniques or scaffolding can provide insight into their impact. Such analysis can be done on both poetic assessments and non-poetic assessments alike. As an educator, you should gather and evaluate samples of relevant assessments and projects completed before any poetry interventions are introduced. These can then be compared to similar student work after poetic scaffolding, analysis, or creation has been integrated. Doing so allows you to discern what effects specific poetry-related interventions, assignments, and scaffolds may have had on student skills and learning, and where they might be adjusted going forward. However, poetry's effects on motivation, enjoyment, and

emotional engagement can be more difficult to quantify, though no less important. The multilayered nature of poetry means its effects do not always fit a simple 'before and after' evaluation. While surveys can provide useful data, also recognise that poetry's influences on students' personal growth and wellbeing may be revealed in more intangible ways over time.

- **Educator observations.** As an educator, you can document your own observations about shifts in student motivation, retention, collaboration, and other key variables before and after integrating poetry. For example, you may notice increased engagement during poetry discussions or more meaningful retention of concepts explored through poetry. As well as using Chapter 5 to help guide you on any poetic reflections, you might also consider tracking indicators like participation rates, attendance, and energy levels, and the impact poetry does or does not have on these.

When conducting and analysing the data generated using these methods, you should be guided by the approaches laid out in Chapter 4, including the need for informed consent, safeguarding, and potentially seeking formal ethical approval from your institutes' ethical review board (or equivalent). Particularly if you wish to publish your findings.

These evaluative methods should be conducted during the lifetime of the module or course itself, rather than solely at the end, to directly benefit the current students through timely adjustments, not just to inform future iterations. By gathering data from students while they are currently engaged, educators can pivot approaches to optimise poetry's value for those same learners.

To fully assess students' development of competencies, you should try to collect data from multiple relevant sources using a range of different approaches. It is also ideal to conduct evaluations at multiple points over time, rather than just once, to track progress and growth. Triangulating findings from diverse data sources and time periods allows for a more comprehensive analysis of competency attainment (Nygaard and Belluigi, 2011).

Present your evaluations in a clear and engaging manner that has intrinsic value for students, rather than framing them as compulsory or overly formal. If students feel 'surveyed out', they may resist participating fully, skewing results, or diminishing future response rates (Schwarz and Struhkamp, 2007). Make evaluation activities interactive, meaningful, and even fun. For example, set aside class time for structured focus groups with refreshments provided; framing evaluation as an integral part of the learning journey prevents fatigue and elevates responsiveness.

Incorporating students actively in the process of articulating and measuring the impact of your approach can significantly enhance the evaluation phase. This participatory approach aligns well with the principles of participatory action research, where students are not just passive subjects but active contributors in assessing the effectiveness of educational interventions (Halliday et al, 2019). By involving students in designing surveys, interpreting data, and even in conducting focus groups, they gain a sense of ownership and deeper insight into the learning process. This method not only enriches the data collected but also fosters a collaborative learning environment where students' voices are valued and their feedback directly influences the evolution of any poetic integration.

When involving students in any research activities, the ethics process needs to be very carefully considered (see Chapter 4). This includes seeking formal ethical approval from your institution's ethical review board, ensuring informed consent from all participants, and safeguarding sensitive information. You should also provide clear guidelines on confidentiality and the responsible use of data. Additionally, when students are involved in the research process, discuss these ethical considerations, making them aware of the responsibilities and standards expected in academic research. This not only ensures ethical compliance but also educates students on the critical aspects of conducting research, an invaluable skill in their academic and professional development.

EXERCISE 6.2: EVALUATING YOUR POETIC PRACTICE

Estimated engagement time: Varies over multiple teaching cycles (approximately one academic term to a year).

Aim: To evaluate and refine the integration of poetic techniques in teaching practices through a data-driven approach.

Objectives:

- Collect comprehensive data on the impact of poetic techniques on student learning and engagement.
- Analyse collected data to identify strengths and areas for improvement.
- Implement refinements based on findings and re-evaluate for continuous pedagogical enhancement.

Output: An evaluated and refined approach to integrating poetry in teaching practices, documented findings, and an action plan for continuous improvement.

Type of exercise: Individual evaluation and refinement.

Materials needed:

- Survey creation tools (such as Google Forms, SurveyMonkey).
- Student work samples (including poetry drafts, discussion posts, assignments, journals, essays).
- Observational notes.
- Access to a platform for conducting focus groups or interviews (such as Zoom, Microsoft Teams).
- Data analysis tools (spreadsheet software, qualitative analysis software).

Activity:

Step 1: Gather data

As an educator, you can use several methods to collect evaluative data on the impact of poetic techniques in your classroom. Conduct student surveys at multiple points, before and after poetry integration, to get their feedback. These surveys should encompass both quantitative measures, such as rating scales, and qualitative avenues, like open-ended questions, to capture a holistic understanding of student feedback. However, it is paramount to exercise caution and strategic timing to avoid inducing survey burnout, which could potentially compromise the validity and richness of the responses. Hold focus groups or interviews to gain more in-depth qualitative insights from a sample of students. Review relevant student artefacts such as poetry drafts, discussion posts, assignments, journals, and essays. Compare samples of student work before and after poetry integration to assess growth and document your own observational notes tracking metrics like participation, motivation, comprehension, and collaboration.

Step 2: Analyse and integrate findings

Review survey results and focus group responses to identify patterns in student responses and summarise perceptions of what worked well versus areas needing improvement. Alongside this, you might analyse student assessments for observable evidence of poetry's impact on skills like critical thinking, retention, and creativity over time. In doing so, consider your own observational notes on such factors as engagement and learning, using these to formulate a well-rounded assessment of poetry's benefits and limitations.

Step 3: Identify refinements

Use your analysis to pinpoint areas needing refinement and additional support. For example, identify needs for more scaffolding for struggling students, addressing misconceptions, improved activity alignment to outcomes, or the opportunity for more collaborative projects. Consider modifications to your approach that could enhance poetry's impact for both your learners and the wider institution.

Step 4: Implement changes

Based on these areas for improvement, make enhancements to the way in which you integrate poetry into your practice. This might include providing more educator modelling, adding scaffolds for challenging concepts, or designing more effective rubrics to support your assessments. As you are making these adjustments you should always try to address any misconceptions revealed through student feedback.

Step 5: Repeat evaluation

After making refinements, repeat the evaluation process through follow-up surveys, focus groups, assessment reviews, and observations. Re-evaluate your practice periodically to assess what has worked well, and to identify any new areas needing modification for continuous improvement.

Sustaining the momentum

As we outlined at the start of this chapter, integrating poetry into higher education is an ongoing journey requiring active maintenance and cultivation. To fully realise poetry's potential, educators must strategically sustain momentum within their spheres of influence. This necessitates continuously expanding poetry's presence through collaborations, scholarly activity, and personal development.

An essential first step is to establish clear goals to guide your continued efforts. Begin by setting manageable goals for poetry integration over the next year. Additionally, plan professional development goals to enrich your own growth as a poetic practitioner over time. Dedicating time to regularly read, analyse, write, attend conferences on, and take creative courses in poetry will build your fluency and confidence in implementing poetic techniques across educational contexts. With clear goals guiding your progress on both a professional and personal level, you will be well-positioned to actively expand and sustain poetry's integration.

Some examples of manageable goals could include:

- Start every taught session in a module with an introductory poem over the next academic year.
- Submit a study to a peer-reviewed journal on student outcomes using poetic inquiry methods by the end of next year.
- Facilitate monthly optional poetry writing workshops for students starting in the next academic term.
- Complete an online poetry writing course by the end of this academic year.

Starting with small, achievable milestones builds confidence and momentum. As indicated with the last example listed, we also encourage you to set manageable goals for your own continued growth as a poetic practitioner.

To support you on your journey, you can also join or initiate communities exploring poetic approaches to teaching and research. Such communities provide valuable inspiration, feedback, and support to persist in your efforts (Petrich et al, 2013). Here are some ideas for you to consider:

- Connect with local collectives, colleagues, or social media networks related to your field and interests. Follow educators who are integrating poetic techniques and share your own ideas and resources. These connections offer sounding boards and windows into others' experiences.
- Look for avenues to collectively advance poetry's educational roles through collaborative projects. For example, co-author articles, case studies, or book chapters with colleagues documenting poetic interventions and their impacts. You might also develop conference presentations or workshops showcasing your initiatives and inviting discussion.
- Consider pursuing internal or external funding opportunities to conduct wider studies on poetry's academic benefits within your institution or beyond. Seek partners across departments or institutions to propose larger scale research.
- Start a regular poetry group with colleagues focused on pedagogical applications where you can share, workshop, and peer review poetic teaching tools and resources.

Leveraging the power of community provides continuity. These collective initiatives create visibility, inspire others, push boundaries, and generate momentum to help sustain and evolve poetic practices in higher education.

EXERCISE 6.3: PLANNING YOUR POETIC DEVELOPMENT

Estimated engagement time: Varied, ongoing (Initial planning may take 1–2 hours; subsequent reflections and refinements are ongoing).

Aim: To articulate clear goals and develop a structured action plan for integrating poetry into teaching, research, and personal professional development, with a focus on continuous improvement and sustainability.

Objectives:

- Set manageable goals for integrating poetry into teaching, research, personal growth, and collaborations.
- Develop a detailed action plan outlining steps, resources, and timelines to achieve these goals.
- Establish a routine for reflecting on progress, refining goals, and seeking feedback for continuous improvement.

Output: A comprehensive poetic development plan with articulated goals, an action plan, and a reflective practice for ongoing refinements.

Type of exercise: Individual planning and reflection.

Materials needed:

- Writing materials (notebook, computer).
- Access to resources for professional development (such as training workshops, mentors, online communities, collaborative projects).

Activity:

Step 1: Articulate your goals

- Teaching goals. Set one or two manageable goals for integrating poetic techniques into your teaching over the next year. What new approaches will you introduce and what do you hope to achieve?
- Research goals. Outline specific goals for building poetry into your academic research. Will you analyse poems as data, compose poetic works related to your field, or incorporate student poetry as part of your ethnography?
- Personal growth goals. Note professional development goals to expand your own knowledge, skills, and comfort with poetry to enrich your practice. What skills do you need to cultivate, and where can you go to do this?
- Collaboration goals. Identify communities, partnerships, or collaborative projects that could support your continued poetry integration. Which connections will you pursue, and how might you best share your own practice and experience?

Step 2: Develop an action plan

Break down each of your goal categories into manageable action steps that specify required tasks and optimal timelines. For each step, detail the resources and supports you may need to accomplish it successfully, whether materials, funding, technology, training, mentors, or partnerships. Organise the action steps into a comprehensive plan, clarifying your poetic pathway for achieving both short- and long-term goals over the next 1 or 2 years.

Step 3: Reflect and refine

Revisit your goals and action plan frequently, updating them based on your learnings, experience, and growth with poetry integration. Adjust timelines or steps as needed. Where possible, share your goals with trusted colleagues, mentors, or partners. Their feedback can help refine goals to be most meaningful. Nurture mutual commitment and growth. Use reflection to ensure your goals stay relevant to your evolving needs and aspirations. Allow this plan to be a living document that guides your continued poetic journey.

The future of poetry in higher education

As our expedition through poetry's potential draws to a close, it is fitting that we look to the road ahead. What does the future hold for poetry and its expanding roles within higher education? While challenges remain, there are increasing glimmers of light signifying a shifting ethos towards more enlightened, inventive educational practices where poetry finds a welcoming home.

Enduring scepticism poses perhaps the greatest challenge impeding poetry's integration in higher education. Some academic communities may harbour doubts about poetry's academic value and maintain a perception of it as impractical or insubstantial. However, the sheer breadth of studies validating poetry's pedagogical and research advantages, including the cases profiled in this book, provide ample justification to counter such doubts.

Educators already convinced of poetry's merits must proactively address scepticism by highlighting benefits strongly aligned to institutional priorities. For instance, you might emphasise poetry's capacity to build transferable skills sought by employers, such as creativity, critical analysis, and communication (Norton and Gregson, 2020). Similarly, you could draw links between poetry and university diversity and inclusion goals, based on poetry's ability to elicit multiple perspectives and highlight marginalised voices (Illingworth et al, 2018).

Those daring to incorporate poetic techniques despite initial hesitation serve as the frontiers for change. Although starting small in scope, their visible modelling of poetry methods signals possibilities to others. These initiatives grant permission for poetry, gradually expanding its perceived legitimacy, with each lesson, assignment or publication helping to sew change from within existing systems.

These bottom-up, grassroots efforts are key drivers of poetry's expanding foothold, even within resistant academic cultures. Their courage to exercise agency with small steps of experimentation, reflection, and adjustment have the potential to gradually transform poetry from anomaly to norm.

At the structural level, academic institutions must also demonstrate openness to creative innovations that disrupt conventional methodologies. Reward systems valuing narrow measures of prestige and output will need reconfiguration to recognise the methods outlined in this book as being on a par with other, more quantitative approaches. Institutions should continue to offer promotion and reward pathways for educators who undertake influential pedagogical innovation and leadership in areas like poetry as a medium for learning and teaching, recognising its ability to enrich teaching and learning. Poetry's role necessitates embracing inclusive definitions of knowledge and challenging hegemonic academic power dynamics. Leading creative advancements like poetry integration should be valued by institutions as part of education-focused career progression.

Of course, poetry's flourishing future presence is only one facet of the larger cultural renewal needed in higher education. To blossom, poetry requires an academic ecosystem centred on wisdom, ethics, and growth of humanity's full potential. But poetry also reciprocally contributes to this revival through its capacities for perspective-taking, meaning-making, and reflection.

Poetry affords us the opportunity, both individually and collectively, to script a new narrative for higher education where creativity, individuality, and diversity replace speed, performativity, and standardisation. What exciting developments will we witness when poetry is unleashed from the margins to permeate academia's very core?

Further study

As you continue your poetic journey beyond this book, here are some recommended activities to deepen your exploration:

Create a poetry reading/writing group. Join or start a group of like-minded colleagues interested in further developing poetic techniques. Meet regularly to read, analyse, and create poems together. Discuss applications to your educational contexts and use writing prompts and exercises to nurture your skills.

Develop a poetic reflective practice. Commit to writing short reflective poems periodically to process experiences, insights, or emotions related to your practice. These could be teaching reflections, research insights, or personal growth poems. Compile them into a journal to track your development.

Experiment with poetic feedback. Try providing a student or colleague with poetic written feedback on a non-poetic assessment, instead of prose comments. Reflect on their reaction and the extent to which this might offer any additional insight into your use of poetry.

Facilitate a poetic workshop. Prepare and deliver a conference workshop or development session guiding others in effectively using poetry in their own higher education contexts.

Propose a special issue. Suggest a special issue of a journal in your field exploring poetry's emerging relevance across disciplines. Use this as a platform to spotlight poetic research and curate a collection advancing understanding of poetry's multifaceted applications.

Final reflections

As we reach these final pages, we hope you feel empowered, enlightened, and emboldened. In writing this book, we set out to illuminate poetry's immense potential to enrich teaching, research, assessment, reflection, and growth in higher education. Through diverse examples, pragmatic strategies, and reflective prompts, we have shown some ways in which you might cultivate this potential within your own practice.

In exploring poetry's potential to enrich teaching and research in higher education, our deeper hope is that this book has also served as an invitation to welcome poetry more fully into your own life. Beyond its instrumental applications, poetry holds immense personal value. Through lyrical language and imaginative expression, poems speak to our shared humanity, nurture wisdom, and cultivate meaning. Engaging with poetry not only shapes us as educators but nourishes us as human beings. It offers a lens through which to appreciate life's complexity and beauty amidst the demands of academia. We hope the possibilities outlined in this book inspire you to make space for poetry, both professionally and personally – to let its rhythm infuse your work and its wonder fill your spirit.

To all who joined us on this journey, we extend our deepest appreciation. We thank you for your openness to see poetry in a new light within the hallways of higher education. Your willingness to reflect, experiment, and innovate gives us tremendous hope. The higher education landscape evolves one educator, one student, one activity at a time – through the collective creativity of pioneers like you.

The true impact of this book will be realised through your actions. As you integrate poetic activities into your teaching, leverage poems in your research, and nurture your inner poet through reflective writing, you make these ideas tangible. We cannot wait to hear your stories of poetry's blossoming influence in your corners of higher education. Please continue to share your experiences with us and others. It is in this co-learning that our collective and poetic wisdom truly expands.

With gratitude and optimism for
the promising path ahead,
Sam and Kirsten

Notes

five

1 Vogdes, N.L. (1980) 'Snowbound', *Social Work*, 25(1): 67. Reprinted by permission of Oxford University Press.

2 "A Gift," by Denise Levertov, from *Sands of the Well* (1996). Reprinted by permission of New Directions Publishing Corp.

References

Acim, R. (2023) 'Virtual poetry, nursing and Google Meet', *Journal of Poetry Therapy*, 36(4): 286–99.

Anderson, A., Rezamand, P., and Skibiel, A.L. (2022) 'Effects of wildfire smoke exposure on innate immunity, metabolism, and milk production in lactating dairy cows', *Journal of Dairy Science*, 105(8): 7047–60.

Aird, R.E. (2017) 'From impostership to mastersness: Experiences of a postgraduate student's transition to higher education reflected through poetry', *Journal of Research in Nursing*, 22(6–7): 522–32.

Alterio, M. and McDrury, J. (2003) *Learning Through Storytelling in Higher Education: Using Reflection and Experience to Improve Learning*, London: Routledge.

Ashford-Rowe, K., Herrington, J., and Brown, C. (2014) 'Establishing the critical elements that determine authentic assessment', *Assessment & Evaluation in Higher Education*, 39(2): 205–22.

Bali, M. and Zamora, M. (2023) 'Designing and adapting for community with Intentionally Equitable Hospitality', in T. Jaffer, S. Govender and L. Czerniewicz (eds) *Learning Design Voices*, EdTech Books, pp 179–94.

Barnett, R. (2000) 'University knowledge in an age of supercomplexity', *Higher Education*, 40: 409–22.

Baron, P. and Corbin, L. (2012) 'Student engagement: Rhetoric and reality', *Higher Education Research & Development*, 31(6): 759–72.

Belvis, E., Pineda, P., Armengol, C., and Moreno, V. (2013) 'Evaluation of reflective practice in teacher education', *European Journal of Teacher Education*, 36(3): 279–92.

Berg, M. and Seeber, B.K. (2016) *The Slow Professor: Challenging the Culture of Speed in the Academy*, Toronto: University of Toronto Press.

Biggs, J. (1996) 'Enhancing teaching through constructive alignment', *Higher Education*, 32(3): 347–64.

Bolton, G. (2014) *Reflective Practice: Writing and Professional Development* (4th edn), London: Sage.

Bourke, B. (2014) 'Positionality: Reflecting on the research process', *The Qualitative Report*, 19(33): 1–9.

Brown, S.A. (2015) 'Creative expression of science through poetry and other media can enrich medical and science education', *Frontiers in Neurology*, 6(3): 1–5.

Brown, S.A. (2019) 'Poetic science: Bidirectional reflection in science and medicine', *The Permanente Journal*, 23(3): 17–177.

Camangian, P. (2008) 'Untempered tongues: Teaching performance poetry for social justice', *English Teaching: Practice and Critique*, 7(2): 35–55.

Campbell, F., Jack, K., and Rogers, H.A. (2022) 'Qualitative exploration of existing reflective practices used by undergraduate dental students in paediatric dentistry', *Dentistry Journal*, 10(1). DOI: 10.3390/ dj10010001.

Campo, R. (2020) 'What poetry means for doctors and patients in a pandemic', *Wired*, [online] 3 August, Available from: www.wired.com/story/what-poetry-means-for-doctors-and-patients-during-a-pandemic/

Candy, L. (2019) *The Creative Reflective Practitioner: Research Through Making and Practice*, London: Routledge.

Carless, D. and Boud, D. (2018) 'The development of student feedback literacy: Enabling uptake of feedback', *Assessment & Evaluation in Higher Education*, 43(8): 1315–25.

Carless, D., Salter, D., Yang, M., and Lam, J. (2011) 'Developing sustainable feedback practices', *Studies in Higher Education*, 36(4): 395–407.

Carter, D. (2013) *Teaching Poetry in the Primary School: Perspectives for a New Generation*, London: Routledge.

Celly, K.S. (2009) 'Creative writing in marketing education: Poetry as an innovative pedagogical tool', *Marketing Education Review*, 19(1): 65–71.

Chan, Z.C. (2013) 'Exploring creativity and critical thinking in traditional and innovative problem-based learning groups', *Journal of Clinical Nursing*, 22(15–16): 2298–307.

Chan, Z.C.Y. (2017) 'Poetry writing and artistic ability in problem-based learning', *International Journal on Disability and Human Development*, 16(1): 37–44.

Chavis, G.G. (2011) *Poetry and Story Therapy: The Healing Power of Creative Expression*, London: Jessica Kingsley Publishers.

Cole, T.R., Carlin, N.S., and Carson, R.A. (2015) *Medical Humanities: An Introduction*, Cambridge: Cambridge University Press.

Collins, B. (1996) *The Apple that Astonished Paris*, Fayetteville, AR: University of Arkansas Press.

Combs, G. and Freedman, J. (1990) *Symbol, Story and Ceremony: Using Metaphor in Individual and Family Therapy*, New York: Norton.

Cranton, P. (2016) *Understanding and Promoting Transformative Learning: A Guide to Theory and Practice*, Virginia: Stylus.

Cranton, P. and Carusetta, E. (2004) 'Developing authenticity as a transformative process', *Journal of Transformative Education*, 2(4): 276–93.

Creely, E. (2018) 'What's poetry got to do with it? The importance of poetry for enhancing literacy and fostering student engagement', *Literacy Learning: The Middle Years*, 26(3): 64–70.

Creely, E., Henderson, M., and Henriksen, D. (2019) 'Failing to succeed: The value of failure in creativity', in *Society for Information Technology and Teacher Education International Conference*, March, Association for the Advancement of Computing in Education, pp 1403–11.

Cronin, C. and Hawthorne, C. (2019) '"Poetry in motion" a place in the classroom: Using poetry to develop writing confidence and reflective skills', *Nurse Education Today*, 76: 73–7.

Dahl, M., Guillet de Monthoux, P., and Helin, J. (2022) 'The poetic teaching space: Gaston Bachelard and a third realm in management education', *Culture and Organization*, 28(3–4): 362–77.

Davin, L., Tejero, J.M., Simmons, T., Shaham, D., Borvon, A., Tourny, O., et al (2023) 'Bone aerophones from Eynan-Mallaha (Israel) indicate imitation of raptor calls by the last hunter-gatherers in the Levant', *Scientific Reports*, 13(1). DOI: 10.1038/s41598-023-35700-9.

Day, L. (2018) 'Reflective poetry: Beautiful baby and reflection', *Whitireia Nursing & Health Journal*, 25: 91–4.

De Vita, G. and Case, P. (2003) 'Rethinking the internationalisation agenda in UK higher education', *Journal of Further and Higher Education*, 27(4): 383–98.

Dewey, J. (1933) *How We Think: A Restatement of the Relation of Reflective Thinking to the Educative Process*, Boston: D.C. Heath and Company.

Donaldson, D.P. (2001) 'Teaching geography's four traditions with poetry', *Journal of Geography*, 100(1): 24–31.

Elbelazi, S.A. and Alharbi, L. (2020) 'The "exotic other": A poetic autoethnography of two Muslim teachers in higher education', *Qualitative Inquiry*, 26(6): 661–6.

English, A.R. (2016) 'John Dewey and the role of the teacher in a globalized world: Imagination, empathy, and "third voice"', *Educational Philosophy and Theory*, 48(10): 1046–64.

Evans, A., Cody, A., Copeland, A., Giddings, J., Joy, P.A., Noone, M.A., et al (2017) 'Reflective practice: The essence of clinical legal education', in A. Evans, A. Cody, A. Copeland, J. Giddings, P.A. Joy, M.A. Noone, et al (eds) *Australian Clinical Legal Education: Designing and Operating a Best Practice Clinical Program in an Australian Law School*, Canberra: The Australian National University Press, pp 153–77.

Faherty, A. (2015) 'Developing enterprise skills through peer-assessed pitch presentations', *Education + Training*, 57(3): 290–305.

Faulkner, S.L. (2016) *Poetry as Method: Reporting Research Through Verse*, London: Routledge.

Feinstein, P. (2007) *Willow Pattern*, Nottingham: Five Leaves Publications.

Fiore, M. (2015) 'Pedagogy for liberation: Spoken word poetry in urban schools', *Education and Urban Society*, 47(7): 813–29.

Foster, W. and Freeman, E. (2008) 'Poetry in general practice education: Perceptions of learners', *Family Practice*, 25(4): 294–303.

Fox, J. (1997) *Poetic Medicine: The Healing Art of Poem-Making*, New York: Putnam.

Frost, R. (1916) *Mountain Interval*, New York: H. Holt and Company.

Frost, R. (1928) *West-Running Brook*, New York: Henry Holt and Company.

Furman, R. (2004) 'Using poetry and narrative as qualitative data: Exploring a father's cancer through poetry', *Families, Systems and Health*, 22(2): 162–70.

Furman, R. (2014) 'Beyond the literary uses of poetry: A class for university freshmen', *Journal of Poetry Therapy*, 27(4): 205–11.

Gibbs, G. (1988) *Learning by Doing: A Guide to Teaching and Learning Methods*, Oxford: Further Education Unit.

Giroux, H. (2020) *Critical Pedagogy*, Wiesbaden: Springer Fachmedien.

Golafshani, N. (2003) 'Understanding reliability and validity in qualitative research', *The Qualitative Report*, 8(4): 597–607.

Gómez, M. (2022) 'Engaging with historically marginalized voices through blackout poetry', *Social Studies Research and Practice*, 17(2): 218–28.

Gura, E.G. (1992) 'Relativism', *Curriculum Inquiry*, 22(1): 17–23.

Halliday, A.J., Kern, M.L., Garrett, D.K., and Turnbull, D.A. (2019) 'The student voice in well-being: A case study of participatory action research in positive education', *Educational Action Research*, 27(2): 173–96.

Hanauer, D.I. (2012) 'Meaningful literacy: Writing poetry in the language classroom', *Language Teaching*, 45(1): 105–15.

Haskins, C.H. (2002) *The Rise of Universities*, New Brunswick, NJ: Transaction Publishers.

Healy, D and Smyth, S. (2017) 'Poetry as an engagement strategy: A novice teacher experience of its use within lectures', *Nurse Education in Practice*, 24: 43–8.

Hiley, T.J. (2006) 'Finding ones voice: The poetry of reflective practice', *Management Decision*, 44(4): 561–74.

Howe, K.R. and Berv, J. (2000) 'Chapter II: Constructing constructivism, epistemological and pedagogical', *Teachers College Record*, 102(7): 19–40.

Huisman, B., Saab, N., van den Broek, P., and van Driel, J. (2019) 'The impact of formative peer feedback on higher education students' academic writing: A meta-analysis', *Assessment & Evaluation in Higher Education*, 44(6): 863–80.

Huye, H. (2015) 'Using poetry and art analysis to evoke critical thinking and challenging reflection in senior-level nutrition students', *Journal of Nutrition Education and Behavior*, 47(3): 283–5.

Ice, P., Swan, K., Diaz, S., Kupczynski, L., and Swan-Dagen, A. (2010) 'An analysis of students' perceptions of the value and efficacy of instructors' auditory and text-based feedback modalities across multiple conceptual levels', *Journal of Educational Computing Research*, 43(1): 113–34.

Iida, A. (2008) 'Poetry writing as expressive pedagogy in an EFL context: Identifying possible assessment tools for Haiku poetry in EFL freshman college writing', *Assessing Writing*, 13(3): 171–9.

Illingworth, S. (2016) 'Poetry in Higher Education: An Investigation into its Potential for Fostering Student Engagement', Master's Thesis, Manchester Metropolitan University.

Illingworth, S. (2020) 'Creative communication: Using poetry and games to generate dialogue between scientists and nonscientists', *FEBS Letters*, 594(15): 2333–8.

Illingworth, S. (2021) *A Sonnet to Science: Scientists and Their Poetry*, Manchester: Manchester University Press.

Illingworth, S. (2022) *Science Communication Through Poetry*, Cham: Springer International Publishing.

Illingworth, S. (2023a) 'Poetry as a device to distil science', in S. Rowland and L. Kuchel (eds) *Teaching Science Students to Communicate: A Practical Guide*, Cham: Springer International Publishing, pp 193–7.

Illingworth, S. (2023b) 'Using poetry to actively target the incubation period', in O. Varsou (ed) *Teaching, Research, Innovation and Public Engagement*, Cham: Springer International Publishing, pp 109–19.

Illingworth, S. and Radhakrishnan, M.L. (2023) '"I am here because I wanted to shine": How poetry can be used to better understand undergraduate students' first-year chemistry or related course experiences', *Chemistry Education Research and Practice*, 24: 868–81.

Illingworth, S. and Grimwood, M. (2024) 'Learned words: How poetry can be used to reflect on staff belonging in higher education', *Journal of Further and Higher Education*. DOI: 10.1080/0309877X.2023.2301006

Illingworth, S., Bell, A., Capstick, S., Corner, A., Forster, P., Leigh, R., et al (2018) 'Representing the majority and not the minority: The importance of the individual in communicating climate change', *Geoscience Communication*, 1(1): 9–24.

Jack, K. (2015) 'The use of poetry writing in nurse education: An evaluation', *Nurse Education Today*, 35(9): e7–10.

Jack, K. (2017) 'The meaning of compassion fatigue to student nurses: An interpretive phenomenological study', *Journal of Compassionate Health Care*, 4: 1–8.

Jack, K. (2022) 'Demonstrating empathy when communicating with older people', *Nursing Older People*, 34(1): 34–41.

Jack, K. and Wibberley, C. (2014) 'The meaning of emotion work to student nurses: A Heideggerian Analysis', *International Journal of Nursing Studies*, 51(6): 900–7.

Jack, K. and Illingworth, S. (2017) '"Saying it without saying it": Using poetry as a way to talk about important issues in nursing practice', *Journal of Research in Nursing*, 22(6–7): 508–19.

Jack, K. and Illingworth, S. (2019) 'Developing reflective thinking through poetry writing: Views from students and educators', *International Journal of Nursing Education Scholarship*, 16(1). DOI: 10.1515/ijnes-2018-0064.

Jack, K. and Illingworth, S. (2023) 'Rehearsing empathy: Exploring the role of poetry in supporting learning', *Arts & Health*. DOI: 10.1080/17533015.2023.2256361.

Januchowski-Hartley, S.R., Sopinka, N., Merkle, B.G., Lux, C., Zivian, A., Goff, P., et al (2018) 'Poetry as a creative practice to enhance engagement and learning in conservation science', *BioScience*, 68(11): 905–11.

Jawaheer, M. (2023) 'A self-study of my parallel journey of unlearning and relearning using blackout poetry in a literature didactics module', *Studying Teacher Education*, 19(1): 24–43.

Johns, C. (2010) *Guided Reflection: A Narrative Approach to Advancing Professional Practice* (2nd edn), Chichester: Wiley Blackwell.

Johnston, C.R., Caswell, D.J., and Armitage, G.M. (2007) 'Developing environmental awareness in engineers through Engineers Without Borders and sustainable design projects', *International Journal of Environmental Studies*, 64(4): 501–6.

Joshi, A., Paralikar, S., Kataria, S., Kalra, J., Harkunni, S., and Singh, T. (2022) 'Poetry in medicine: A pedagogical tool to foster empathy among medical students and health care professionals', *Journal of Poetry Therapy*, 35(2): 85–97.

Keleş, U. (2023) 'Exploring my in-betweenness as a growing transnational scholar through poetic autoethnography', in B. Yazan, E. Trinh, and L.J.P. Herrera (eds) *Doctoral Students' Identities and Emotional Wellbeing in Applied Linguistics*, London: Routledge, pp 67–79.

Kelly, R. (2006) *May Day*, Canada: Parsifal Press.

Kesselring, T. and Müller, U. (2011) 'The concept of egocentrism in the context of Piaget's theory', *New Ideas in Psychology*, 29(3): 327–45.

Kolb, D.A. (1984) *Experiential Learning: Experience as the Source of Learning and Development*, Englewood Cliffs: Prentice Hall.

Korstjens, I. and Moser, A. (2018) 'Series: Practical guidance to qualitative research. Part 4: Trustworthiness and publishing', *European Journal of General Practice*, 24(1): 120–4.

Kossman, S. (2005) 'Authentic assessment for RN students: Writing case studies and teaching projects', *Journal of Nursing Education*, 44(2): 96.

Krom, C.L. and Williams, S.V. (2011) 'Tell me a story: Using creative writing in introductory accounting courses to enhance and assess student learning', *Journal of Accounting Education*, 29(4): 234–49.

Kumagai, A. (2017) 'Beyond "Dr. Feel-Good": A role for the humanities in medical Education', *Academic Medicine*, 92(12): 1659–60.

Kumagai, A.K. and Wear, D. (2014) '"Making strange": A role for the humanities in medical education', *Academic Medicine*, 89(7): 973–7.

Ladenheim, M. (2014) 'Engaging Honors students through newspaper blackout poetry', *Honors in Practice*, 10: 45–53.

Lahman, M.K. and Richard, V.M. (2014) 'Appropriated poetry: Archival poetry in research', *Qualitative Inquiry*, 20(3): 344–55.

Langer, C.L. and Furman, R. (2004) 'Exploring identity and assimilation: Research and interpretive poems', *Forum Qualitative Sozialforschung/Forum: Qualitative Social Research*, 5(2). DOI: 10.17169/fqs-5.2.609.

Leavy, P. (2020) *Method Meets Art: Arts-Based Research Practice*, New York: Guilford Publications.

Levertov, D. (1996) *Sands of The Well*, New York: New Directions.

Lizzio, A. and Wilson, K. (2008) 'Feedback on assessment: Students' perceptions of quality and effectiveness', *Assessment & Evaluation in Higher Education*, 33(3): 263–75.

Macfarlane, B. (2015) 'Student performativity in higher education: Converting learning as a private space into a public performance', *Higher Education Research & Development*, 34(2): 338–50.

Majorana, J. and VanDeusen, E. (2022) 'Promoting emotional well-being in the university classroom through poetry', *About Campus*, 27(2): 26–34.

Manley, S. (2018) 'Home-made poetry as pedagogical tool: An experience from the law classroom', *English in Education*, 52(3): 213–24.

Maree, J.G. (2022) 'The psychosocial development theory of Erik Erikson: Critical overview', in R. Evans and O.N. Saracho (eds) *The Influence of Theorists and Pioneers on Early Childhood Education*, London: Routledge, pp 119–33.

Maretic, S. and Abbey, H. (2021) '"Understanding patients' narratives": A qualitative study of osteopathic educators' opinions about using Medical Humanities poetry in undergraduate education', *International Journal of Osteopathic Medicine*, 40: 29–37.

Marino, M.C. (2020) *Critical Code Studies*, Cambridge, MA: MIT Press.

Marlow, M.J. (2015) 'Does Kingsfield live? Teaching with authenticity in today's law schools', *Journal of Legal Education*, 65(1): 229–41.

Marrou, H.I. (1982) *A History of Education in Antiquity*, Madison, WI: University of Wisconsin Press.

Maryani, I., Martaningsih, S.T., and Bhakti, C.P. (2017) 'Module based on pedagogical content knowledge to increase the engagement and skills of the future teachers in designing a lesson plan', *Journal of Education and Learning*, 11(1): 91–102.

Matthews, M. (2022) 'Creativity in the lives of English teachers: Voices through found poetry', *English in Education*, 56(4): 357–71.

Mazza, N. (2022) *Poetry Therapy: Theory and Practice* (3rd edn), London: Routledge.

McArthur, J. (2023) 'Rethinking authentic assessment: Work, well-being, and society', *Higher Education*, 85(1): 85–101.

McFadyen, J. and McCullagh, J. (2015) 'Design collaborations: The good, the bad, and the unthinkable', *Design Principles and Practices: An International Journal – Annual Review*, 8(1): 17–29.

Meehan, M. (2002) 'Open forms of narrative', in B. Walker (ed) *The Writer's Reader: A Guide to Writing Fiction and Poetry*, Rushcutter's Bay: Halstead Press, pp 23–8.

Mezirow, J. (1997) 'Transformative learning: Theory to practice', *New Directions in Adult and Continuing Education*, 74: 5–12.

Millar, V. (2016) 'Interdisciplinary curriculum reform in the changing university', *Teaching in Higher Education*, 21(4): 471–83.

Mood, L. (2018) 'Poetry: An innovative teaching strategy for exploring empathy with beginning nursing students', *Journal of Nursing Education*, 57(5): 315–18.

Morgan, C., Lange, K., and Buswick, T. (2010) *What Poetry Brings to Business*, Ann Arbor, MI: The University of Michigan Press.

Morris, J.A., Urbanski, J., and Fuller, J. (2005) 'Using poetry and the visual arts to develop emotional intelligence', *Journal of Management Education*, 29(6): 888–904.

Mueller, J. (2005) 'The authentic assessment toolbox: Enhancing student learning through online faculty development', *Journal of Online Learning and Teaching*, 1(1): 1–7.

Nguyen-Truong, C.K.Y., Davis, A., Spencer, C., Rasmor, M., and Dekker, L. (2018) 'Techniques to promote reflective practice and empowered learning', *Journal of Nursing Education*, 57(2): 115–20.

Nicol, D., Thomson, A., and Breslin, C. (2014) 'Rethinking feedback practices in higher education: A peer review perspective', *Assessment & Evaluation in Higher Education*, 39(1): 102–22.

Nilon, R. (2020) 'Poetic license: Using documentary poetry to teach international law students paraphrase skills', *InSight: A Journal of Scholarly Teaching*, 15: 142–56.

Norton, F. and Gregson, M. (2020) 'The thinking skills deficit: What role does a poetry group have in developing critical thinking skills for adult lifelong learners in a further education art college?', *Education Sciences*, 10(3): 73.

Nygaard, C. and Belluigi, D.Z. (2011) 'A proposed methodology for contextualised evaluation in higher education', *Assessment & Evaluation in Higher Education*, 36(6): 657–71.

Ojose, B. (2008) 'Applying Piaget's theory of cognitive development to mathematics instruction', *The Mathematics Educator*, 18(1): 26–30.

Osowiecka, M. and Kolańczyk, A. (2018) 'Let's read a poem! What type of poetry boosts creativity?', *Frontiers in Psychology*, 9: 1781.

Ostrom, R., Gotesman, M., and But, J.C. (2020) 'Poetry in biology: Enhancing science education with creative writing', in J.C. But (ed) *Teaching College-Level Disciplinary Literacy*, Cham: Palgrave Macmillan, pp 103–18.

Park, J.H., Kim, J.Y., and Kim, H.O. (2022) 'Effects of a group poetry therapy program on stress, anxiety, ego-resilience, and psychological well-being of nursing students', *Archives of Psychiatric Nursing*, 41: 144–52.

Parker, J.D.A., Saklofske, D.H., Wood, L.M., and Collin, T. (2009) 'The role of emotional intelligence in education', in J.D.A. Parker, D.H. Saklofske, and C. Stough (eds) *Assessing Emotional Intelligence*, Boston, MA: Springer, pp 239–55.

Parker, M. and Jary, D. (1995) 'The McUniversity: Organization, management and academic subjectivity', *Organization*, 2(2): 319–38.

Pennebaker, J.W. and Evans, J.F. (2014) *Expressive Writing: Words that Heal*, Washington: Idyll Arbor.

Petrich, M., Wilkinson, K., and Bevan, B. (2013) 'It looks like fun, but are they learning?', in M. Honey and D.E. Kanter (eds) *Design, Make, Play: Growing the Next Generation of STEM Innovators*, Abingdon: Routledge, pp 50–70.

Pollack, A.E. and Korol, D.L. (2013) 'The use of Haiku to convey complex concepts in neuroscience', *Journal of Undergraduate Neuroscience Education*, 12(1): A42–8.

Prendergast, M. (2006) 'Found poetry as literature review: Research poems on audience and performance', *Qualitative Inquiry*, 12(2): 369–88.

Quinlan, K.M. (2016) *How Higher Education Feels: Commentaries on Poems That Illuminate Emotions in Learning and Teaching*, Cham: Springer.

Quinlan, K.M. (2021) 'Towards an educational humanities for teacher education: Building the relational, emotional, and ethical bases of teaching practice', *Oxford Review of Education*, 47(6): 752–69.

Ramsden, P. (2003) *Learning to Teach in Higher Education*, London: Routledge.

Rashidi, K., Ashktorab, T., and Birjandi, M. (2022) 'Impact of poetry-based ethics education on the moral sensitivity of nurses: A semi-experimental study', *Nursing Ethics*, 29(2): 448–61.

Roberts, M. (2010) 'Emotional intelligence, empathy and the educative power of poetry: A Deleuzo-Guattarian perspective', *Journal of Psychiatric and Mental Health Nursing*, 17(3): 236–41.

Roberts, S.K., Brasel, N.A., and Crawford, P.A. (2014) 'Poetry as praxis: An exploration of poetry discourse as qualitative inquiry', *Journal of Poetry Therapy*, 27(4): 167–81.

Robinson, S.A. (2017) '"Me Against the World": Autoethnographic poetry', *Disability & Society*, 32(5): 748–52.

Rose, D.H., Harbour, W.S., Johnston, C.S., Daley, S.G., and Abarbanell, L. (2006) 'Universal design for learning in postsecondary education: Reflections on principles and their application', *Journal of Postsecondary Education and Disability*, 19(2): 135–51.

Rudolph, J., Tan, S., and Tan, S. (2023) 'ChatGPT: Bullshit spewer or the end of traditional assessments in higher education?', *Journal of Applied Learning and Teaching*, 6(1). DOI: 10.37074/jalt.2023.6.1.9.

Rule, A.C., Carnicelli, L.A., and Kane, S.S. (2004) 'Using poetry to teach about minerals in earth science class', *Journal of Geoscience Education*, 52(1): 10–14.

Sanchez, S. and Brown, T. (2023) 'Introducing poetic collage as method: From the voices of girls of color', *Cultural Studies ↔ Critical Methodologies*, 23(2): 193–203.

Sarauw, L.L. and Madsen, S.R. (2020) 'Higher education in the paradigm of speed: Student perspectives on the risks of fast-track degree completion', *Learning and Teaching*, 13(1): 1–23.

Schön, D.A. (1991) *The Reflective Practitioner*, Farnham: Ashgate Publishing.

Schwarz, C. and Struhkamp, G. (2007) 'Does evaluation build or destroy trust? Insights from case studies on evaluation in higher education reform', *Evaluation*, 13(3): 323–39.

Shapiro, J. (2010) 'Take 2 poems and call me in the morning: Reading medically themed poetry for insight and renewal', *Journal of Science Communication*, 17(11): 1–6.

Shapiro, J., Kasman, D., and Shafer, A. (2006a) 'Words and wards: A model of reflective writing and its uses in medical education', *Journal of Medical Humanities*, 27(4): 231–44.

Shapiro, J., Rucker, L., Boker, J., and Lie, D. (2006b) 'Point-of-view writing: A method for increasing medical students' empathy, identification and expression of emotion, and insight', *Education for Health: Change in Learning & Practice*, 19(1): 96–105.

Sherman, N. (2014) 'Recovering lost goodness: Shame, guilt, and self-empathy', *Psychoanalytic Psychology*, 31(2): 217–35.

Simecek, K. and Rumbold, K. (2016) 'The uses of poetry', *Changing English*, 23(4): 309–13.

Simonsmeier, B.A., Peiffer, H., Flaig, M., and Schneider, M. (2020) 'Peer feedback improves students' academic self-concept in higher education', *Research in Higher Education*, 61: 706–24.

Smart, F. (2014) 'Poetic transcription: An option in supporting the early career academic?', *Journal of Perspectives in Applied Academic Practice*, 2(3): 66–70.

Smart, F. (2017) 'Poetic transcription with a twist: An approach to reflective practice through connection, collaboration and community', *Innovations in Education and Teaching International*, 54(2): 152–61.

Smart, F. and Loads, D. (2017) 'Poetic transcription with a twist: Supporting early career academics through liminal spaces', *International Journal for Academic Development*, 22(2): 134–43.

Smith, S., Akhyani, K., Axson, D., Arnautu, A., and Stanimirova, I. (2021) 'Learning together: A case study of a partnership to co-create assessment criteria', *International Journal for Students as Partners*, 5(2): 123–33.

Snow, C.P. (2012) *The Two Cultures*, Cambridge: Cambridge University Press.

Stageberg, N.C. and Anderson, W.L. (1952) *Poetry as Experience*, New York: American Book Company.

Svenaeus, F. (2018) 'Edith Stein's phenomenology of sensual and emotional empathy', *Phenomenology and the Cognitive Sciences*, 17: 741–60.

Threlfall, S.J. (2013) 'Poetry in action [research]. An innovative means to a reflective learner in higher education (HE)', *Reflective Practice*, 14(3): 360–7.

Thunig, A. and Jones, T. (2021) '"Don't make me play house-n★★★er": Indigenous academic women treated as "black performer" within higher education', *The Australian Educational Researcher*, 48: 397–417.

Timmins, F., Murphy, M., Howe, R., and Dennehy, C. (2013) '"I hate Gibb's reflective cycle 1998" (Facebook©2009): Registered nurses' experiences of supporting nursing students' reflective practice in the context of student's public commentary', *Procedia – Social and Behavioral Sciences*, 93: 1371–5.

Trowler, V. (2019) 'Transit and transition: Student identity and the contested landscape of higher education', in S. Habib and M.R.M. Ward (eds) *Identities, Youth and Belonging: Studies in Childhood and Youth*, Cham: Palgrave Macmillan, pp 87–104.

Van der Pol, J., Van den Berg, B.A.M., Admiraal, W.F., and Simons, P.R.J. (2008) 'The nature, reception, and use of online peer feedback in higher education', *Computers & Education*, 51(4): 1804–17.

Vogdes, N.L. (1980) 'Snowbound', *Social Work*, 25(1): 67.

Vygotsky, L.S. (1978) *Mind in Society: The Development of Higher Psychological Processes*, Cambridge, MA: Harvard University Press.

Wakeman, B.E. (2013) *Knowing Through Poetic Reflection*, Brighton: Pen Press.

Walder, A.M. (2017) 'Pedagogical innovation in Canadian higher education: Professors' perspectives on its effects on teaching and learning', *Studies in Educational Evaluation*, 54: 71–82.

Walshe, N. (2017) 'An interdisciplinary approach to environmental and sustainability education: Developing geography students' understandings of sustainable development using poetry', *Environmental Education Research*, 23(8): 1130–49.

Wardle, A. and Illingworth, S. (2022) 'GC Insights: Geoscience students' experience of writing academic poetry as an aid to their science education', *Geoscience Communication*, 5(3): 221–5.

Webster, D. (2010) 'Promoting empathy through a creative reflective teaching strategy: A mixed-method study', *Journal of Nursing Education*, 49(2): 87–94.

Wild, F., Marshall, L., Bernard, J., White, E., and Twycross, J. (2021) 'UNBODY: A poetry escape room in augmented reality', *Information*, 12(8): 295–315.

Wiley, D., Bliss, T.J., and McEwen, M. (2014) 'Open educational resources: A review of the literature', in J. Spector, M. Merrill, J. Elen, and M. Bishop (eds) *Handbook of Research on Educational Communications and Technology*, New York, NY: Springer, pp 781–9.

Wiliam, D. (2011) *Embedded Formative Assessment*, Solution Tree Press.

Winstone, N.E. and Carless, D. (2020) *Designing Effective Feedback Processes in Higher Education: A Learning-Focused Approach*, Abingdon: Routledge.

Winstone, N.E., Nash, R.A., Parker, M., and Rowntree, J. (2017) 'Supporting learners' agentic engagement with feedback: A systematic review and a taxonomy of recipience processes', *Educational Psychologist*, 52(1): 17–37.

Whittle, B., Macgregor, K., Cooper, M., Sornalingam, S., and Okorie, M. (2022) 'Can poetry help GPs and GP trainees to develop their reflective practice?', *InnovAiT*, 15(6): 323–9.

Wright, J.K. (2003) 'Writing for protection: Reflective practice as a counsellor', *Journal of Poetry Therapy*, 16(4): 191–8.

Zamora, M., Bali, M., Mehran, P., and Cronin, C. (2021) 'Equity unbound as critical intercultural praxis', *The Journal of Applied Instructional Design*, 10(4). DOI: 10.59668/329.5270.

Zhang, K. (2020) 'Learning the "language" of motherhood as international graduate students: A poetic ethnography', *Art/Research International: A Transdisciplinary Journal*, 5(2): 309–44.

Zhang, K. (2021) 'Embrace the uncontrolled nature of poetry writing: A poetic ethnographic study on international graduate student mothers' intercultural discourses', *Qualitative Inquiry*, 27(3–4): 429–43.

Index

References to case studies and exercises appear in *italic* type; those in **bold** type refer to tables.

Q

R

Printed in the USA
CPSIA information can be obtained
at www.ICGtesting.com
JSHW011536020624
64077JS00003B/5

9 781447 372295